SHE THINKS LIKE A BOSS - LEADERSHIP

9 ESSENTIAL SKILLS FOR NEW FEMALE LEADERS IN BUSINESS & THE WORKPLACE. HOW TO INFLUENCE TEAMS EFFECTIVELY & COMBAT IMPOSTER SYNDROME

JEMMA ROEDEL

CONTENTS

INTRODUCTION

I wrote this book *She Thinks Like a Boss* because I felt there was a gap in the market. As a female in business, many self-help and business books simply ignore our struggles and challenges. Sure, women in the workplace experience many of the same things men do. But often, the challenges are more specific to us as women. If you, like me, want advice on how to think and act like *the* boss, then this book is for you.

Before writing this book, I wondered about things like:

- What makes female executives successful? Are there traits common to all of them?
- What leadership style is best for women in business? What challenges do women face in leadership?
- How do we as women identify problems and solve them?
- How do I develop a high-performing team?
- Does anyone else feel imposter syndrome? Self-doubt? How do we overcome this?
- How do I instil and grow confidence not only in myself but in my team?
- Which communication skills are most important?
- How should I handle negotiations?
- How do we transform fear into action?

Perhaps you have wondered about similar things in the past. This book will cover each of those questions. Each chapter focuses on a trait that will help you think like a boss, from:

- Personality styles
- Leadership skills
- Coaching skills
- Negotiation
- Communication skills

- Banishing doubt
- Overcoming fear.

In Chapter 1, we will discuss the following traits which successful women have in business:

- Confidence
- Accountability
- Leadership
- Innovation
- Creative Thinking
- Vision
- Having a Long-Term View
- Viewing Failure as Opportunity
- Focusing on Self-Development
- Knowing Your Worth
- Strategic about Complaints
- Team Players
- Building Relationships
- Raising You Hand to Lead
- Asking for Promotions
- Seeking Opportunities

Chapter 2 focuses on the difference between leadership and management and common leadership challenges. I'll also address micromanagement.

Chapter 3 addresses typical stumbling blocks for female leaders, including:

- Lack of Confidence
- Inequitable Treatment
- Not Speaking Up
- Not Having Influential Relationships at Work
- Being a Perfectionist
- Lack of Problem-Solving Skills
- Not Knowing Your Leadership Style

Chapter 4 delves into how to build out a high-performance team. This chapter will be particularly impactful for those in hiring positions or for women who manage other people. I'll address characteristics of high-performing teams - things to think about as you're building out your team, and how to motivate your managers.

In Chapter 5, I address how to overcome self-doubt and imposter syndrome, things many women feel in the workplace.

Chapter 6 expands beyond this to address how to build confidence in yourself and your team. I'll show you how to build self-confidence, convey confidence, and explain the difference in confidence between men and women generally.

Chapter 7 provides an overview of communication secrets of the most successful women. We'll address some commonly known communication differences between men and women, discuss potential pitfalls, and share communication tips and tricks that you might consider using in the workplace.

Chapter 8 is all about the art of negotiation. I'll share negotiation tactics as well as some spoken and unspoken rules of negotiation.

In our final chapter, Chapter 9, we'll talk about something that many people don't want to address: fear. I want you to be able to transform fear into action! We'll acknowledge that even the most successful women feel fear through specific examples, and I'll share tips on how to overcome specific types of fear that you might find in the workplace.

Throughout the book, I will also reinforce my personal experience with research and data so that you know that we're not in this alone! My hope is that you find what resonates with you in this book and start implementing it in your own life.

That is ultimately my goal with this book. No matter where you are on the corporate ladder or what your specific challenges are right now, you will find many pieces of advice to help you turn those challenges into opportunities. I recommend that you slowly incorporate the tips and tricks mentioned in this book. Then, measure the results and tweak them as needed. Remember that only you know your situation best, so take what resonates with you and leave the rest. No matter what, please consider passing the book on or recommending it to another woman when you are done. We're all in this together. Here's to being successful in business and learning to think like a boss! Join our community She Thinks Like a Boss : A Community For Business Women on Facebook to discuss any points in the book. We would love to hear from you.

1

WHAT MAKES SOMEONE SUCCESSFUL?

Have you ever looked at a successful woman and thought to yourself . . . how did she get to where she is today? What was it that allowed her to succeed? If so, this chapter is for you. Knowing the common personality traits and habits for success will allow you to not only notice them in other women but also establish habits that help promote these traits in your own life. Now, it's important to know that there is no one roadmap for success. Success is not guaranteed, and what made one person successful can be repeated by another only to result in a different outcome. In this chapter, you will learn what the most common traits and habits of successful women are so that you can start incorporating them into your own life. Building a solid foundation of strong habits is key if you want to be successful over time.

Confidence

"You have to have confidence in your ability, and then be tough enough to follow through."

— ROSALYNN CARTER

Confidence may be the number one factor that makes someone successful over the long term. What is confidence? The Merriam-Webster Dictionary describes it as "a feeling or consciousness of one's powers or reliance on one's circumstances." We're going to focus on the "powers" portion of the definition. Self-confidence is quite simply your belief that you can accomplish something on your own (and with the help of your team.) It's your belief in your ability to get things done.

Not every woman is born with confidence. And, unfortunately, life sometimes makes us less confident based on the situations, people, and circumstances we've encountered along the way. Thankfully, though, confidence *is* something that you can work on. You become more confident when you try new things and succeed at them. They don't have to be large things, either. Small wins are great and can be key to building your confidence over time.

Think of a time when you stepped outside of your comfort zone, took a risk, and it worked out. That's a confidence booster. Anytime someone compliments you on your work - indeed a great confidence booster. Perhaps you are being recognized in your daily life for something only you can bring to the table . . . your analytical skills, ability to build a team, or perhaps you're good at having difficult conversations. Those are all things that should grow your confidence over time.

Why is confidence important? According to a Pew Research Study,[1] in both business as well as in politics, female leaders with confidence are more likely to be viewed as "stronger" than those without confidence by male counterparts. The same study discusses differences in what the general public believes about men and women when it comes to leadership traits in both business and politics. Traits like "ambition, decisiveness, and assertiveness" are believed to help men in both politics and business, whereas being emotional in the office can be seen as a liability for women.

The study states that even with acknowledged differences between men and women, most people tend to have "more confidence [in] women's abilities." Women have a "stronger ability to create a respectful and safe working environment (43%) compared to men (5%). Women are also more likely to value people from different backgrounds (35%) compared to men (3%), consider the impact business decisions have on society (33% vs. 8%), provide guidance and mentorship to young employees (33% vs. 9%), and providing fair pay and good benefits (28% vs. 5%)."

There are many things we as women should be confident about! Look at the list above: we are more likely to create a safe and respectful work environment, value people from different backgrounds, consider the impact business decisions are having on the community, provide mentorship and guidance to others, and provide fair pay and benefits. These are all wonderful things to lean into as a female leader yourself or to promote and encourage in those female leaders around you.

Having confidence in yourself and belief in your work will take you very far in business. Many people will doubt you over time, but your belief in your ability to deliver, even despite obstacles and potential setbacks (and, let's be honest, we've all been there!) will put you far ahead of others in the long run.

Leadership

"Leadership is hard to define, and good leadership even harder. But if you can get people to follow you to the ends of the earth, you are a great leader."

— INDRA NOOYI (FORMER CEO, PEPSICO)

Leadership encompasses many areas but knowing how to lead a team is essential to winning in business. It has been said that leadership is truly the ability to influence those around you. Tony Robbins has been quoted as saying that it is the "most important skill that any human being can master."[2] In the same interview, Robbins says that you must "destroy the limitations within your own mind" to become the best leader possible.

Leadership is the ability to lead others toward a shared end goal. You don't have to be the boss to be a leader, but if you're the boss, you'll be expected to lead. Knowing how to obtain buy-in from those around you and beneath you and to get a team to work together toward a common goal is a quality all strong female leaders have.

Accountability

"Responsibility equals accountability equals ownership. And the sense of ownership is the most powerful weapon a team or organization can have."

— PAT SUMMITT, AMERICAN WOMEN'S
COLLEGE BASKETBALL HEAD COACH

Good female leaders are accountable. This means that they follow through on what they say they are going to do, which makes them trustworthy. Businessman Arnold H. Glasgow said, "A good leader takes little more than his share of the blame and little less than his share of the credit." Strong female leaders also hold others accountable. This means that they not only lead by example, but they also expect others to follow. Setting a high standard of accountability means everyone knows that they are responsible for executing; that others are relying on them.

Holding others accountable is also one way for women leaders to empower those on their team. Knowing that a boss is not going to micromanage your work can be fearful for some, but for most people, it gives them a sense of purpose and autonomy that leads to a better end product.

Innovation

"There is no innovation and creativity without failure. Period."

— BRENÉ BROWN

Life is constantly changing and evolving and the ability to innovate is one trait that will set you apart as a leader. Innovation can be anything from establishing a new way of doing something, creating a new product or service based on customer needs, or even something larger like restructuring a portion of a company.

Innovation can even be personal. As an individual, are you fostering innovation in your own life? Is there areas of your life or unchanged habits that had been that same way for one, five, ten years? Perhaps consider trying something new . . . not only to experience something from a different perspective but also to discover if any new insights, self improvement or development come to you as a result of that change.

Encouraging others to innovate is a fast way to empower a team and to show that you want your colleagues and employees to contribute. Great ideas don't only come from the top, and the more you include and welcome ideas to innovate from your team the more you show them how much they are valued and welcome to contribute. They will appreciate this from a leader and create a successful business!

Creative Thinking

"The things we fear most in organizations – fluctuations, disturbances, imbalances – are the primary sources of creativity."

— MARGARET WHEATLEY

Successful women leaders are also creative thinkers. When a problem arises, they do not simply complain about it (ok, sometimes we want to complain for a moment . . .), but after we're done, we find solutions. Many solutions. Creative thinking means thinking "outside of the box." Coming up with new and different ways of approaching something. Harnessing the power of creative thinking will position you as a leader who is nimble, resourceful, and creative. This is especially important because life will constantly bring you new and unique problems. So the ability to come up with solutions that are creative, different, and yet precisely what the business needs will help you stand out as a successful leader.

Vision

"A good leader is able to paint a picture of a vision for the future and then enlist others to go on the journey with her."

— TAMRA RYAN, CEO OF WOMEN'S
BEAN PROJECT

Successful women leaders know how to establish a vision and share it with others. Visionaries are people who can see the big picture and are generally thought of as "idea people." You don't have to be a visionary to be someone who can set a vision.

Setting a vision is being able to inspire those you work with to work toward a common set of values or goals that are important to your organization.

A successful leader inspires others and brings them along on her vision. Anyone successful will tell you that they did not get there alone; there were likely many people along the way who helped. Building the skills needed to not only set a vision for where you want your team to go but then also leading them along over time (through both successes and failures) is the mark of a successful leader.

Having a Long-Term View

"Champions keep playing until they get it right."

— BILLIE JEAN KING, TENNIS
CHAMPION

The most successful women in business have a long-term view of their careers. They know that one job alone will not make or break them and that the mark of a truly successful person in business continues to grow and take on greater responsibility over time. This means beginning with the end in mind—one of the habits recommended in Steven Covey's *7 Habits of Highly Effective People*.

This means that she often will sit down to think about her long-term goals and what skills she would need to get there. Another way to think this through is to objectively view gaps in her resume: what skills would she need to obtain to be eligible for a higher-level position? After determining gaps then she creates daily habits that will support her long-term vision.

Viewing Failure as Opportunity

"Think like a queen. A queen is not afraid to fail. Failure is another stepping stone to success."

— OPRAH

To many people, failures are setbacks that take a long time to recover from. For successful people, failures are simply learning opportunities. The word 'fail' has often been referenced to stand for 'first attempt in learning,' although we know that's not the real definition!

When things do not work out, successful women take the time to determine what went wrong. And then, they apply those learnings to the next time. Because successful people do *not* quit! They try again and again and as long as they are making progress towards their goals, they know that they will reach them eventually in time.

Focus on Self-Development

"Growth and comfort do not coexist."

— GINNI ROMETTY, CEO, IBM

Successful women are constantly working on themselves. They are learning and investing in themselves and their future. This also means that they are extremely self-aware. For things to change, one must acknowledge where they are at now. They truly embrace their strengths, weaknesses, successes, and failures.

Most importantly, they are not afraid to work on anything related to self-mastery. They are always striving for continuous self-improvement, both in their inner and outer worlds. And, they push others around them to do the same.

Knowing Your Worth

"I don't have to be perfect. All I have to do is show up and enjoy the messy imperfect and beautiful journey of mine."

— KERRY WASHINGTON

Because women who tend to be successful are self-aware, they know what they bring to the table in any given situation. This means that they know their value and their worth, and they will not settle for colleagues or positions where they are *not* valued. That's not to say that they don't ever experience setbacks. It's just that as soon as they recognize them, they try to determine if there's something they can do to change the situation and if not, they start to look for another position where their value can be recognized.

Strategic about Complaints

"Leaders think and talk about the solutions. Followers think and talk about the problems."

— BRIAN TRACY, CANADIAN-AMERICAN MOTIVATIONAL SPEAKER, AND SELF-DEVELOPMENT AUTHOR

No job situation is perfect. However, women who are successful in business do not complain about everything. The ones who are the most successful are very strategic about voicing concerns and complaints. Ideally, they address things that are directly impacting their ability to do their job respectfully and openly. And they always propose ideas on ways to solve issues to show that they can be part of the solution as well.

Following on from strategically raising concerns, successful women put forward solutions, not just problems. There is power in being able to call out issues respectfully and helpfully. However, what's even better is when you also offer *potential solutions*, and not just problems.

It is the role of management to block and tackle and make sure that you are well-positioned to do your job and succeed. However, managers are often so busy that they may not even recognize what issues you have to deal with on a day-to-day basis. You can put these challenges on the table but also remember to propose solutions. You will be remembered, most importantly, for being part of the solution and not simply as a "complainer!"

Team Players

"No matter how brilliant your mind or strategy, if you're playing a solo game, you'll always lose out to a team."

— REID HOFFMAN, CO-FOUNDER OF LINKEDIN

At the end of the day, unless you are working for yourself with no employees, you will likely have a team and a boss. This means that the ability to work with people has a direct impact not only on your ability to get things done but also, will likely have an impact on whether you like getting up and going into work each day.

At the beginning of your career, you may think it may not matter whether your peers like you or want to work with you. But as you ascend the corporate ladder it does start to matter, and relationships at the very top are largely about having authority and also the ability to influence and lead teams. You can't lead teams without leading people. And leading people well requires you to show up and be a team player.

There have been many female executives so set on climbing the corporate ladder that they step over everyone to get to the top. Then, they discover that they have no support from below and no friends at work! Don't be this woman. Remember that everyone you work with is a human with real-life issues (just like you) and deserves to be treated with respect. The more you help others succeed the more they will be inclined to help you succeed as well.

They Build Relationships – Not Only Networks

"Success isn't about how much money you make, it's about the difference you make in people's lives."

— MICHELLE OBAMA

Similar to taking a long-term view of one's career, successful women know that networking and building relationships are not a one-time, transactional thing. Successful women know that they will need help and that they should be helping others, too. This means building relationships, not simply networks.

They don't ask: who do I need to know? They ask things like:

- Who needs to know me?
- Who can I help?
- Who can I mentor?
- Who would I like to learn from and work with?

Once they establish connections, they follow up and build relationships over time. A true relationship cannot be forced; it must be authentic and built upon mutual trust and engagement. This means taking an active interest in the life and work of the other person. And sharing knowledge, best practices, and ideas where appropriate.

Raise Your Hand (to Lead)

"What I always say is, 'Do every job you're in like you're going to do it the rest of your life, and demonstrate that ownership of it."

— MARY T. BARRA

Successful people volunteer to lead things when asked. We are all busy, but to truly stand out from the crowd the ability to raise your hand and be willing to lead will set you apart. Also, it shows the leadership in your organization and your management team that you are willing to take on additional responsibility.

Raising your hand allows you to show that you can lead, that you are a team player, and that you are interested in taking ownership over something that could have a positive impact on your organization. Owning a successful project is a very fast way to not only get noticed and make an impact but will also set you up to be considered to climb the corporate ladder quickly.

Ask for Promotions

"We think, mistakenly, that success is the result of the amount of the time we put in at work, instead of the quality of the time we put in."

— ARIANNA HUFFINGTON

How many of us want promotions but have simply never asked for them? One of the reasons that men move up the corporate ladder quicker is that they often are not afraid to ask for what they want. Successful women recognize what they want and boldly go after it.

Asking doesn't mean that we always get what we want. We often may not get it in our desired timing, either. But making your manager aware that you want to be promoted lets them know that you are (likely) also willing to put in the work that will place you in line for that promotion.

Seek Out Opportunities

"There exist limitless opportunities in every industry. Where there is an open mind, there will always be a frontier."

— CHARLES F. KETTERING

Many people are hired to do a job that has a specific role. However, the most successful women go above and beyond what's on their job description. Quite simply: they see problems and issues, and they step up and solve them. This is sometimes called "servant leadership." These are situations that may not normally look like opportunities, but allow you to contribute to your team in many ways outside of what you were hired to do:

- You hear your boss say that she is swamped. Instead of just empathizing with her you ask: "What can I do to help?" or "Is there anything I can take off your plate?"
- You notice that there is a gap between two teams that don't normally work together. You suggest to your boss that you establish a regular catch-up meeting between you and a member of the other team to

facilitate the flow of more regular information and knowledge sharing.

- If you represent your team in a meeting, you share information from those meetings with the rest of your team. You think of the stakeholders who are not in the room and keep an eye open so that the entire team benefits from your presence there.

Also, successful women build networks across organizations and always ask if there is anything they can do to help the other person succeed in their job. This takes the attention off of the individual and shows that they want to help others succeed. Even greater, it shows that you want your organization to succeed as a whole.

In Summary

What makes someone successful is often a unique combination of their personality and situation. However, many of the above traits are commonly seen in successful women across industries. If some of these resonate with you, focus on those skills to enhance them over time. Or, if you recognize anything already part of your personality or leadership style, do whatever you can to build upon these strengths and make them a core part of your leadership style.

2

LEADERSHIP VS. MANAGEMENT AND COMMON LEADERSHIP CHALLENGES

As you can see from Chapter 1, many traits contribute to a strong leader. And no one leader is quite like another. When it comes to leadership there are also many ways you can *be* a leader. Perhaps you'll recognize your style in this chapter. The goal of Chapter 2 is to enable you to recognize the ways that you lead others and to become aware of the potential pitfalls of those styles as well.

Leadership vs. Management

"Management is efficiency in climbing the ladder of success; leadership determines whether the ladder is leaning against the right wall."

— STEPHEN R. COVEY

Leadership and management are not the same things, so it's important to be able to understand the difference. Management is more about managing the day-to-day operations of a business or team. Leadership, however, is ensuring that others are brought into a shared vision and that everyone is working together as a team to achieve those goals.

Whether in a small or large business, for a leader to be successful they must have both management and leadership skills. Leadership skills are also something that you should be constantly working on. According to research by the Chartered Management Institute, 90% of members who completed management and leadership training found that the experience improved their performance at work. If your company offers you leadership training, you may want to take advantage of the opportunity to build and refine your skills or learn new skills that can help you be a stronger leader.

Common Leadership Challenges

Many things trip up new managers. It is easy to succumb to pressure from above and below you when you assume a new role and responsibilities. Below is a list of common pitfalls for managers. Be aware of these and do everything you can not to make them part of your daily routine as they could potentially lead to larger management and team-based issues down the road.

Pride

Congratulations! You've just been promoted. Feels good, doesn't it? Now . . . we have to get to work. Let's not let our pride make us feel like we deserve or are entitled to anything more than we have. Being promoted or assuming a new role with management and leadership responsibilities is a recognition of your capabilities thus far. It means that your management trusts that you can take on more work and larger tasks. This is not the time to believe your own hype. What works instead of pride? Humility and staying humble despite your success. This will ensure that you remain approachable to your colleagues and those you need to manage. And, it will help you build trust and confidence as you ascend the leadership ranks of an organization.

Relying only on yourself

You didn't get to where you are today by yourself, so why would you start ignoring others now? Successful women bring others along with them. If you receive a project to work on or have a goal to reach, ask yourself: who you can bring into the fold to help you? Who is already around you either on your team or otherwise who has the skills that would contribute favourably to this project? A true leader does not succeed by themselves if they work in an organization. Success will be the result of their competence to work with others.

"Teamwork is so important that it is virtually impossible for you to reach the heights of your capabilities or make the money you want without becoming good at it."

— BRIAN TRACEY

If you work solo or own your own business ask yourself what is it that only you can do? What can you delegate or afford to pay someone else to do so that you can focus on what is most impactful? Leaning on others will help immensely—especially when you are at a point where you want to grow and scale your business.

Being fearful

Fear affects everyone differently. For some women, it may prevent them from taking action at all. For others, it could prevent them from admitting they made a mistake when something does not work out. It's normal to have a certain amount of fear if you've taken on a large team or new role. But instead of focusing on that, ask yourself, "Why do I feel this way?" Is it that you feel you don't have the skills required? Or, that you are afraid of failing? Whatever it is, talk to a mentor or coach if you have one. Or, ask your boss to provide the necessary resources if some are lacking and preventing you from successfully performing your full job. Awareness is key.

In her book, *Dare to Lead*, Brené Brown tells us how important it is to acknowledge these feelings when they come up:

> "Rather than spending a reasonable amount of time proactively acknowledging and addressing the fears and feelings that show up during change and upheaval, we spend an unreasonable amount of time managing problematic behaviors."

Brown rightfully acknowledges that often, in an attempt to be "strong," we will try to manage any other issue (literally, anything!) instead of acknowledging our fear. The lesson is clear: acknowledge where you are. Address what may be needed to help you succeed, and bravely and courageously move forward.

Lack of follow through

As you start to rise in an organization, your workload and demands on your time will likely increase. One of the easiest potential pitfalls of leaders is forgetting to follow up or follow through.

If you have an assistant, this is something they can help you with. Make sure that you are consistently touching base with them and that you have set expectations on how they are to help remind you to follow up when needed.

Authors David Norton and Robert Kaplan, in their book *The Balanced Scorecard*, mention that 90% of organizations do not execute their strategies successfully. This can happen for several reasons, but don't let one of those reasons be the fact that you are not following through on the strategies and projects you are managing.

If you do not have an assistant or work solo (or are an individual contributor), then you can still focus on this habit by keeping track of everything you need to follow up on. A simple list will work, and it should be readily accessible (on your phone or computer if needed) and easy to use. Every week or so, take some time to go through your list to see what you still might be waiting on from others, or what information you may owe others. This small habit will immensely help you keep things moving forward and others (who most likely also forget to follow up) will appreciate the reminders.

Not being motivated

It is easy to be motivated when you have a new role. But what happens when the "newness" wears off? Motivation is key to being successful. The truth is that not everyone feels motivated every day. It would probably be impossible to do so! But, once the adrenaline and newness wear off it's up to you to push yourself to show up day after day.

If you've chosen a role for the right reasons, you'll want to show up consistently and continuously. It will be a part of your "why" in choosing this role. However, beyond that, if you are feeling demotivated it can not only affect your desire to show up to work, but it can also affect your work itself as well as your team.

Burning yourself out

As a leader, you will be expected to produce. But don't push yourself so much that you burn out. There is an advisory notice in the safety checklist for airplane safety: "Put your oxygen mask on first before helping other people." This is precisely what you need to do in the office as well. Make sure to take care of yourself first, so that you can take care of others.

What does taking care of yourself look like? It can be anything from traditional self-care like making sure you are getting enough sleep and eating healthy, to things like delegation of tasks and relying on others. Don't push yourself to be the hero or you may end up finding yourself sacrificing things that are important (like your sanity or health). Alternatively, you may find that you do succeed but that it's quite lonely at the top if you tried to do everything yourself.

It's not a weakness to rely on others. It's a strength and a true sign of leadership. It is often said that one should "lead by example." Therefore, one of the best things you can do for your team and those around you is to model what true balance looks like so that success does not come by sacrificing other more important things.

Not being vulnerable

Dr. Brené Brown is a leading expert on vulnerability and leadership. To Brown, vulnerability is "uncertainty, risk, and emotional exposure," and she believes that it is key to being a strong leader. Putting up walls and not being vulnerable seems like something a strong leader would do; however, it is just the opposite that is a true sign of leadership.

Vulnerability and the ability to be one's self in an authentic way will help you truly connect with others you manage and work with. Why? Because being true to yourself and being open with others allows you to build trust with your colleagues—trust that is based in reality and on real connections.

When you are leading people in a business it requires being able to confront difficult situations. Oftentimes, people are afraid to share what is happening because they fear looking weak, ignorant, or as if they don't have things under control. As a leader, when you encounter difficult times, it is an opportunity to lead by example and to be vulnerable with your team. Acknowledge the uncertainty, the potential fear surrounding what is happening, and most importantly how *you* feel. You don't have to go into great detail; simply acknowledging that you too may be experiencing what others are, too, is enough. Being vulnerable allows others to feel like they can open up, too. And this is where true leadership comes in. When you are aware of how people feel and what their daily challenges are, you can help manage the things standing in their way from either doing their job or completing things to the best of their ability. More importantly, continued vulnerability, openness, and transparency help build a foundation for strong relationships over time.

Not understanding how to motivate a team

Understanding how to motivate yourself is one thing. It is something else entirely to understand what it means to motivate others. Here are some things to keep in mind whether you are managing a team, are responsible for someone else's work product, or need to influence people that you work with:

- Everyone is motivated differently: when it comes to motivating teams you should think of it as motivating a group of individuals. What motivates one person is not what motivates someone else. For example, one person may be driven by moving up the corporate ladder, more responsibility, and money.

Another may be motivated by having more vacation time to spend with family. Your goal is to understand how to motivate each person individually while also getting them to buy in and work towards a common goal.

- Motivating a team towards a common goal requires a different skill set entirely: once you understand that each individual is motivated differently now it is your responsibility to get all of these individuals working together towards a common goal. One way to do this is to have something everyone collectively can work towards (i.e., a group goal) and also a way for everyone to "win" when that goal is reached. For example, perhaps you set a goal of your team making profits $500,000 in products and services this quarter. If they reach that goal collectively, everyone will receive a $1,000 bonus.

If you are a new boss or new to managing a team there are a few things you can do in the beginning to give you a head start in building relationships and understanding how people are motivated:

- Schedule one on one time with each person on your team so that you can get to know them extremely well at an individual level.
- Ask what worked and has not worked in the past. This

helps build trust and buy-in, especially if there have been management changes or turnover in the past.

- Don't hold back. Ask what motivates them! Many people have never been asked and may not even know. In that case, ask them what is important to them. You should be able to quickly assess what might motivate them more in their role.

- Determine what you can control and how you can make an impact right away: can you establish a new bonus structure? Reward people with more vacation days? Some of these things may require HR approval so lean into things you have autonomy and decision-making power over in your role.

Lack of prior management experience

There is a heavily cited report on internal hiring from Hewlett-Packard quoted in many books that addresses the gap in confidence that women have compared to men. The report stated that men felt comfortable applying for roles when they met 60% of the criteria whereas women did not feel comfortable applying unless they met 100% of the criteria. This means more women may not apply for jobs that require management experience if they haven't previously managed a team.

Not having previous management experience does not mean you should not manage a team; it simply means you have not done it before. In this case, lean into any resources that are available to you: HR training, mentors, online resources, etc.

Management is simply people management. Think of how you like to be managed; things that good bosses have done in the past and things that have not sat well with you that poor management and bosses have done, as well. Similar to understanding how to motivate individuals, it is important to spend time one on one with each person you'll work closely with to get an understanding of who they are in and out of the office, what's important to them, and to know what areas of expertise they have in the business.

Remember what you bring to the table. You may not have formal management experience, but I bet that you have business experience and expertise in a specific area that brought you to this opportunity. Relationship building is a two-way street. Offer to bring others along in your area of expertise as you lean on them in anything that may be new to you. Don't let the lack of experience stop you from doing your best or wanting to make an immediate impact. Sarah Blakely, the founder of Spanx, says, "Don't be intimidated by what you don't know. That can be your greatest strength and ensure that you do things differently from everyone else." If you remain true to yourself it won't matter if you do not have prior experience. And, you may set a new standard or way of doing things. Something completely different from anything listed in a management book or course—something uniquely you.

Let's talk about micromanaging

The above list is certainly not everything but is a good representative list of issues you may run into on your quest to be a strong leader. Now let's take a moment to talk about one specific area of management that can quickly undermine trust and ruin relationships: micromanaging.

What is micromanaging?

Micromanaging is the act of keeping extremely close eyes on things that you have tried to delegate to others. It can look like checking in on them all the time related to the status of a project, constantly tweaking things and not taking input or recommendations, and any other activity that can be viewed as "hovering."

A recent study by the US-based employer review site Comparably shows that micromanaging is the worst trait that a manager can have according to both the men and women surveyed.[1] People also felt this way regardless of whether they had a male or female manager. 44% of people felt that their male managers were micromanagers vs. 36% of those surveyed who felt their female bosses were micromanagers. This shows that micromanaging is not specific to one gender but rather is often a widespread management issue.

Why do people micromanage?

There are many reasons someone may micromanage. Perhaps you don't trust a colleague's ability to get something done to your standards. You may think you are the only one who knows how to do something "right." Or, perhaps, the project is extremely important, and your reputation is on the line but you won't be doing the heavy lifting. No matter what, it usually has something to do with your reputation and/or a lack of trust in someone else or fear of the project or yourself failing in the long run.

Am I a micromanager?

A 2014 article in the Harvard Business Review titled *Signs That You're a Micromanager*[2] listed out the common traits of a micromanager. Do you recognize any of them in your own life?

- You're never quite satisfied with deliverables.
- You often feel frustrated because you would've gone about the task differently.
- You laser in on the details and take great pride and/or pain in making corrections.
- You constantly want to know where all of your team members are and what they're working on.
- You ask for frequent updates on where things stand.
- You prefer to be CC'd on emails.

If you notice any traits familiar to how you conduct yourself, don't worry! It's possible to overcome being a micromanager. Read on for tips on how to stop micromanaging and build trust with your colleagues.

How to stop micromanaging

The same Harvard Business Review article has suggestions on how to stop micromanaging. They include:

- Getting over yourself: you may know many ways to do something, but that doesn't mean those are the *only* way to do things. If you've hired someone to do something on your team, trust that you hired right and they have a unique background and perspective to get the job done. You may be surprised to find that people *don't* need so much direction and the result may even be stronger as a result of you meddling less!

- Let it go: you have to learn that people can get things done without your hovering over them. Let people surprise you. If you're having a hard time releasing the hold, the article recommends starting with smaller items and moving up to larger, more significant projects.

- Give the "what," not the "how." You do not need to describe in detail how to get everything done. Focus on the result and goal and let your employee figure out the best way to get there. This releases the mental energy that you may be harbouring by worrying about the "best," or "most efficient" way to do something. It also frees you up to focus on larger issues that only you can tackle.

- Expect to win (most of the time): the article states that micromanaging is managing the fear of failure. Does this resonate at all with you? Likely so, if you are a micromanager. You think you can simply do something yourself to have it done "right," or "correctly." While the intention may be rooted in a good place, if you expect to win instead of expecting to fail you may find it easier to delegate tasks without micromanaging.

Moving from micromanagement to management

If you have a desire to move from micromanaging to managing there are some things you can do:

- Talk to your colleagues. Acknowledge your desire to change and ask them to hold you accountable and to give you forgiveness and understanding if you do slip into your old ways.
- Truly let go. Delegate things, focus on the end goal or product and let others take the lead. Leave enough time for edits and brainstorming if needed. You may be surprised to find that some people flourish with a little autonomy and ownership!

- Create space for more. Micromanaging takes a lot of time and energy. If you understand that by giving up on "hovering" behaviours and micromanaging, you are creating space and room for even greater leadership and management opportunities. This may help you to break away from these time-consuming habits.

Recognizing the traits of micromanaging early will help you to curb these habits and will help you create true leadership skills that empower others—leaving you time to deal with issues that only you can tackle. Instead of focusing on how your employees and colleagues are getting things done, redirect your focus to even greater challenges the business is facing, ensuring that you are providing the greatest impact possible to your organization in your role as a leader.

In Summary

This chapter focused on common leadership pitfalls. The important thing is that you are aware of which of these may be prevalent in your leadership style and try to prevent them from becoming a dominant part of how you interact with others. Awareness is key to changing habits. If any traits are common for you, commit to working on those so that you can be the most effective leader possible.

3

STUMBLING BLOCKS FOR FEMALE LEADERS

Inevitably, if you find yourself in a leadership opportunity, you will likely find yourself experiencing challenges over time. This is completely normal. Female leadership in business remains far and few between. According to a 2015 Pew Research Study, female leaders of Fortune 500 companies comprised only 5.2% of all leaders from 1995-2014.[1] This means that the challenges that female leaders face are still unique to a small group of people. In this chapter, I'll highlight some of the common challenges and stumbling blocks for female leaders and how to approach each of them.

Lack of Confidence

Since women occupy smaller percentages of leadership roles overall it is possible to experience "imposter syndrome" or feel less than confident in a role. A recent KPMG study found that 75% of female executives have experienced imposter syndrome in their career.[2] Laura Newinski, KPMG U.S. Deputy Chair and Chief Operating Officer, stated, "It's important to realize that most women experience similar doubts at some point in our careers...our contribution as leaders is pivotal. Together, we have the opportunity to build corporate environments that foster a sense of belonging and lessen the experience of imposter syndrome for women in our workplaces."

Not everyone is going to be a supporter of you in a leadership position. Some people may flat out refuse to help. But that should not stop you. If you struggle with confidence, it's ok to acknowledge these feelings. But make sure to remember your background and experience that qualify you for this current role, what you bring to the table, and what you have to offer your team and your company.

Especially if you do not have supporters in your workspace, make sure to surround yourself with those who know you, love you, and believe in you outside of work. We all need a tribe of people who believe in us. Especially when we may not believe in ourselves. Remember that most people are simply figuring things out as they go along and that your skills and abilities are just as strong as others. You've got this.

Inequitable Treatment

Now more than ever, women are calling upon those in authority to be treated fairly both in and out of the office. While we've always fought for women's rights, it's becoming more and more common to ensure that teams are diverse in terms of gender, background, and experience.

If you believe you are not being treated equitably in any situation, first find your voice. Many people are not even aware that they may be treating others unfairly and unfortunately, many slights are unconscious. Ask for the fairness you deserve, whether it's the right to be considered for an opportunity, or a seat at the negotiation table. Find those who do believe in you and support you and ask them honestly about their thoughts on how you should approach these issues. They may have other ideas that are specific to your situation. And when you can, be sure to bring up other women behind you. Remember what it was like to work your way up the corporate ladder and lead by example when it comes to giving other women opportunities in the workplace.

Not Speaking Up

Let's say that you do have a chance to sit at the table for a meeting or negotiation, but you remain quiet. That's not necessarily a bad thing, but my guess is that you have something to contribute. Whether it's an idea of how to do something differently or to add things to the discussion that should be thought about or considered.

The worst thing one can do is simply to talk for the sake of talking. You don't need to do that! But, when possible, do try to contribute to the conversation in a way that is beneficial for the group. Think about what you can *add* to the discussion. What's missing or needs to be considered? Who is not in the meeting but should provide feedback? What perspective can only you add? Remember that you are in this position and meeting for a reason. How can you enhance it?

Not Having Influential Relationships at Work

In the workplace, it's quite often natural for men to build relationships with other men. But one thing I can recommend when you become a new leader or have a desire to move up the corporate ladder, is to start building relationships with people who have influence. People who are known as "decision-makers."

How do you build these relationships? Naturally. You never want to force a relationship or friendship. Some common ways to start are to notice people for who they are, and not their title or role. Do you have similar hobbies? Do you live in the same area? Anything else in common?

Then, encourage yourself to step out of your comfort zone and invite these people individually to either coffee or lunch. Learn more about what they do and share what your role is as well.

Remember that the most meaningful connections are a two-way street. Is there anything you can share with them that would help them in their role as well?

Being a Perfectionist

Some people may think that being a perfectionist is a sign that you like things done correctly. And yes, while that is generally how perfectionists feel, in the workplace perfectionism can be detrimental to your brand as a leader.

Why? Perfectionism leads to micromanaging which can plummet team morale. It also doesn't make you perfect; it makes you difficult to work with and could potentially label you as someone who is not a team player.

If you identify as a perfectionist, what are some ways that you can overcome these tendencies?

- Delegate small projects to team members.
- Acknowledge these tendencies to someone you trust and ask them to hold you accountable as you try to change over time.
- Only allow two revisions maximum to a document so as not to put pressure on colleagues to have unlimited revisions.
- Relax! Do whatever you need to approach work differently.
- Live by the motto, "Done is better than perfect."

Lack of Problem-Solving Skills

One thing you are certain to encounter as a female leader is problems! Life is full of them and the exciting thing is that you're unlikely to be able to anticipate some, if not most of them, daily. Because of this, it is good to have a framework for dealing with any potential problems or issues that may arise.

Understanding how men and women view problems

According to the Keller Institute, men and women see problems differently. In a blog post[3] about these differences, they wrote:

> "Men look at problems and see one thing. That one
> thing which needs correction, and they seek to fix it.
> Women look at the same problem and see multiple
> things that need fixing. Men use their left brain
> searching for the answer, while women use their right
> brain searching for several answers."

Understanding that men and women view issues differently is the first step to working with your male colleagues on issues. Knowing that they literally approach problems differently and only may see one as opposed to many issues can be helpful.

What does this mean for you? It means that you can help your male colleagues by creating an 'issue list' that needs to be tackled. One at a time, methodically. That way they do not become overwhelmed by multiple issues, and you can help them focus on all that needs to be resolved instead of the one issue they may be focusing on.

How smart women solve problems

In the same article, the Keller Institute lays out a five-step process that smart women can use to solve problems:

1. **Define the problem that's not the squeaky wheel**: What does this mean? This simply means that you need to find out what the core issue or core problem is. While there might be many surface-level problems, there is likely an underlying or core problem that is the source of many problems. For example, if someone is overspending and going into debt, buying too much of something for which they already have extras at home, and not feeling great about her finances, the core problem may be that she does not have a monthly budget. This would allow her to focus on how she wants to spend her money each month, encourage her to take stock of what she has on hand, and help with feelings of anxiety related to her finances. A solution to one core problem solves *all* of the issues. So, seek out the core, or deeper problem.

2. **Get everyone involved**: This is stereotypically a woman's strength—community and collaboration. When you find out a core problem, determine who else may have an invested interest in this being solved?

Why? Because they, too, may have thoughts of how best to resolve it. In the case of the budget above, perhaps the woman has a partner with whom she lives and splits finances. This partner may want to provide feedback on the budget itself, what budgeting software they may want to use, or thoughts on how it should be maintained moving forward. Ask who else may need to be involved in creating this solution.

3. **Look everywhere for answers**: Do not limit yourself to only one solution or even one way of looking for a solution. You can, of course, do whatever comes naturally to you. Do you seek out wise counsel from those who have been there before? Do you go to the library or the internet? Do you ask friends, colleagues, other stakeholders? Whatever it is, seek out answers as much as you can in as many varied places as you can. This allows you to ensure that whatever final answer you land on is well thought out and tested against multiple sources. It also helps you to learn from the mistakes and mishaps of others—saving yourself from having to do that, too!

4. **Make a top ten list**: Make a list of ten potential solutions to your issue. Then, try them out *before* you implement them. The article from the Keller Institute says that you will save a lot of time with this step. Focus on what stands out to you as a really strong solution and go from there. Test it out. If it doesn't

work, try something else. When you do find
something that works, move on to the next step.

5. **Decide, implement, and evaluate**: Quickly
decide and implement and then evaluate your solution.
You can be quick in this step as long as you've done the
thought and testing that is in Step 4. Always feel free to
evaluate how things are going and then tweak as
needed.

Working through this framework will help you confidently
address challenges and problems that may arise, using your
unique strengths and skill sets as a female leader to evaluate, test
solutions, and solve problems more quickly.

Not Knowing Your Leadership Style

Can you accurately and succinctly describe how you lead others?
If not, review the following types of leadership styles to see if
any resonate with you. When you assume new leadership roles
and positions, being able to articulate how you lead others and
work with a team will allow your new teammates and direct
reports to more quickly be able to adapt to your leadership in a
time of transition. It may also help you notice any potential
working challenges based on other personality types as you get
to know your colleagues. Here are five common types of
leadership styles:

The "Hands-Off" Leader

Are you someone who loves to empower others and the mere thought of micromanaging makes you cringe? You may be a "hands-off" leader. That doesn't mean that you're not there when people have questions or need guidance. Simply that you prefer to let others worry about *how* they get things done. You don't feel the need to watch over their shoulder or critique every step that they complete.

If you are a hands-off leader here are a few tips to manage your team more effectively:

- Acknowledge that this is your leadership style. Ask if anyone requires more regular check-ins or feedback. If so, plan accordingly.
- Show people the end goal and desired result and let them manage how they get it done.
- Make sure to let your team know that you have an 'open door' should anyone have questions or need advice. You don't want them to feel abandoned.
- Check in prior to the end deadline so that if someone has gone way off track or simply gone in a different direction there is time to course-correct and guide them to the appropriate end goal.
- Empower your team to make decisions and be clear about what aspects you want to be consulted on.

Working for a hands-off manager can be fun and empowering for the right person. The important thing is to be upfront about this style and make sure it works well with those you manage.

The Controlling Leader

Perhaps you are someone who has a hard time letting go and delegating. Or, maybe you work in an area where the entire end product is a reflection on you personally, regardless of who on your team worked on it. If you are the type of person that likes to direct and know what everyone is working on at all times, you may be a controlling leader. It's not necessarily a bad thing as long as you acknowledge your style and are able to communicate this to others.

Controlling leaders are only able to relax when they know that people understand what is expected of them and they can trust that people are going to follow through on what they say they are going to do. This means that if you are a controlling leader and you assume a new team, it will take time to establish this trust. Here's how to handle a new team if you are a controlling leader:

- Acknowledge how important work is to you in front of your team. Controlling leaders often value their work product and see it as a reflection of themselves personally. Conveying this to others will help them understand where you are coming from.
- Be honest about your tendencies to micromanage and

control. People will be more understanding when you acknowledge it upfront.

- Instead of micromanaging, establish clear check-in schedules. This allows you the comfort of knowing you'll be able to check in and gives your team the comfort of understanding that even though there will be more check-ins you won't be micromanaging.

The "By the Book" Leader

If you work in the military, on a production line, or in another structured environment, you may consider "by the book" leadership. This style of leadership does not leave a lot of room for personalizing the way you manage others, and the ultimate goal is that everyone operates according to policy and procedure.

Usually, policies and procedures are put in place for a reason. It can be the health and safety of others (like in a production line), or to ensure that everyone is held to the same standards (as in the military). Either way, being able to articulate the standards and the "why" behind them will help you be an effective leader in these types of settings.

Leadership in these settings will often be different than if you are working in a small business or a larger corporate environment. Much of your management responsibilities will be to ensure that everyone is following the standards put in place and that they are adhering to all policies. As much as you can, if you can maintain a sense of humanity while in this leadership style it will help your direct reports see you as someone who cares about them rather than simply pushing an agenda.

Transformative Leader

Perhaps your team or division is going through a period of change or preparing for future shifts in the business. This may call for transformative leadership, where you push people beyond their comfort zones so that everyone can grow together. Transformative leaders inspire hope in others and can walk with them, side by side, through uncertainty and even times of upheaval.

Especially in times of change, transformative leaders can keep teams grounded, steering the overall corporate ship while everyone focuses on what needs to be done. They are there if anyone needs assistance and guidance and even encouragement but ultimately their strongest asset is in inspiring a team to achieve something wildly beyond what everyone could have done individually.

The Collaborative Leader

Are you the type of person who wants everyone on your team to feel included? To feel like they can contribute to decision-making processes? You may be a collaborative leader.

Collaborative leaders are constantly obtaining feedback to see how their teams are doing and to consider different viewpoints and perspectives. They know that by making decisions in a silo they are potentially alienating people they work with and who work for them. They are usually open leaders who want to make sure the voice of the collective is heard.

If you are a collaborative leader here are a few ways to make your team feel included:

- Establish a weekly check-in where everyone can share what their priorities are and what they are working on.
- Have one on one meetings with those who report to you and also people who report to your direct reports (called "step down" meetings).
- Have a brainstorming board where anyone can contribute ideas. Make sure they are discussed on a bi-weekly or monthly basis.
- Have a complaint jar: an anonymous complaint jar where people can complain about things without fear of retribution. For those things that can be acted upon, take the time to fix or solve the issues.

Do any of the above leadership styles resonate with you? Are there any that are new to you but which you could implement in your job? Anything you'd like to change or do differently? The best leaders recognize their unique style. It can be a combination of any of the above or something that simply comes naturally to you. What is important is that it helps you lead others well and encourages the team to reach a common goal.

In Summary

As a leader, it is important to understand things that commonly cause stumbling blocks as well as to understand your leadership style. Awareness is key for both of these areas within leadership. When you are aware of the things that are areas of weakness you can either work on them to make them strengths, or substitute habits that promote strong leadership.

Understanding your leadership style within your industry and work environment will help you guide your team more clearly, as well as understand how you might approach management and collaboration among your team. It will help you communicate your expectations as well, which allows your team to understand where you are coming from and gives them a chance to not only meet those expectations but to potentially also exceed them. A true win-win!

Take our quiz to find out what type of leader you are at, www.shethinkslikeaboss.com

DEVELOPING A HIGH-PERFORMANCE TEAM

A successful female leader can only do so much alone. At some point, you may be asked to lead a team, and/or if you work for yourself, your business might get to a point where you need to hire a team to scale and grow. This chapter is all about how to develop and build a high-performance team. We'll discuss how teams can help a business be successful as well as how to motivate your team to increase productivity.

What is a high-performance team?

Many businesses today are successful because their leaders knew how to put together, grow, and manage high-performing teams. You may be asking yourself: what *is* a high-performance team? At its core, it is a team of people that excels: they set, reach, and exceed goals consistently and they are key to helping a business move forward.

Simplilearn, an online educational technology company in San Francisco, California, describes[1] high-performance teams as:

> *"A high-performance team is a group of highly skilled people working in cross-functional areas and who focus on achieving a common business goal. The team is aligned with and committed to shared values and vision and work towards a common objective. This highly effective team is innovative in problem-solving and is known for displaying a high level of communication and collaboration, delivering consistent and superior results."*

How to build a high-performance team

Now that you know what a high-performance team is you may be asking yourself how to put one together. You cannot simply put skilled people together and expect them to perform, as a group, at the highest levels. There is some planning and resources that are necessary.

The first thing you should plan for is to diversify your team in terms of skill set: *who* is strong at *what*? You don't need three people on your team who are all financial geniuses. One person who can do the financial modelling and notice risks ahead of time should be enough so that you can build out your team with people who bring other skills to the table.

Also, the members of the team should be able to articulate the skill sets of others just as well as they can articulate their own. Why? This is so that they know who to go to, and when, and so that they understand when to pull others into a project or to solve a problem that has arisen. Even though people may have different skill sets, all team members work together towards a common goal. This is what makes high-performance teams extremely effective.

Characteristics of High-Performance Teams

High-performance teams often have certain characteristics that contribute to their success:

1. *They are effective*

As we mentioned earlier, high-performance teams are effective. They have defined output that is impactful to the organization. As you are putting a team together ask yourself:

- What is the ultimate goal for this group? What would define success?
- What skills are needed to make sure a team hits these goals?
- What personality types might you need on this team?
- Are there one or more people on this team who can drive things forward in your absence (if needed)?

Another part of being effective is being efficient. The team has little duplication in terms of skill sets and output. People know and understand what they are responsible for in terms of contribution and the rest of the team knows what others are contributing. That way, no two people are working on the same things. This makes a team more effective and efficient.

2. The processes put in place work for the team

As you start assembling your team, you'll have to put processes in place that help your team work together and communicate effectively. Here are some questions to consider as you implement processes:

- Is your team mostly remote or do they live in the same area? This may affect whether you do mostly virtual or in-person meetings.
- What are the mediums by which you normally like to communicate? Text, phone, email, etc?
- Do you have a project management system where you can administer tasks and monitor progress?
- How does the team best like to work?
- How often do you want to check in and how often would it help your team to check in? Sometimes, your team might want you to check in more often if changes are being made or if it is a time of uncertainty for your business.

It is a good idea to gather your team together in the beginning after formation to discuss these things. Obtaining your team's input will allow you to hear from them directly and tweak any processes based on their feedback. It will also encourage them to and have ownership over the processes, which makes them more likely to support any process that is formally implemented.

3. Everyone shares the same vision

This is the true power of a high-performance team. Everyone is working under the same vision and moving in the same direction. Here are a few ways you can encourage your team to get excited about a shared vision:

- If the vision has not yet been established, consider including the team in creating the vision.
- Place the vision in a common area or in a place where all employees can see it daily.
- Explain upon creation of the team what your idea for the vision is so that people know and understand what they are working towards.
- Ensure that you only put people on your team who also believe in the vision.

4. Transparent and open communication

According to Cynthia Burggraf Torppa, Ph.D. and Extension Educator of Family and Consumer Sciences at Ohio State

University Extension, "women tend to be the relationship specialists and men tend to be the task specialists."[2] Men and women simply communicate differently. As a female leader, you have a unique ability to build relationships as well as drive the business forward based on needs.

As you build your high-performance team, consider the types of communication styles of those on your team. Are they more "fact" based? Do they need to know the "why" behind things? Consider all of this as you establish the following communication parameters:

- How often do you want "check-ins" from your team?
- How often do you want your team to meet?
- Do you want each person on the team to be aware of what others are working on? (We would recommend this!)
- How will people be able to alert others of potential issues?
- How will you share general information and questions?
- What is the culture of communication on your team? Open? Transparent? Does communication generally come only from the top (i.e., Executives) or can it come from anyone?

What's most important is that all members of the team feel valued and included and also that they feel like they are heard.

Think through these items related to communication as you build out your high-performance team.

Considerations as you're forming your team

Now that we've gone over the top characteristics of high-functioning teams, we'll review things you should keep in mind as you build out your team.

1. The size is key

According to a McKinsey article[3] on high-performing teams, "team composition is the starting point." A smaller team seems to work better, however, you don't want it to be too small (the article points out that less than "six" might be too small) because it implies that there might be a lack of diversity. Similarly, effectiveness is also diminished if the team is too big, say "larger than ten."

Based on McKinsey's research, a team between seven to nine seems to be a sweet spot, allowing for diversity and autonomy but also different options when it comes to succession planning and likely a variety of skill sets to choose from as projects arise.

2. The team should share the same values

As you select members of your team don't try to fit people into it that simply do not fit well. When team members feel free to interact freely and without hesitation, trust is formed over time. There is a fine line between sharing values and a common goal and accidentally falling into groupthink. It is the role of a successful manager to navigate this and to prevent groupthink from happening.

Joseph Falkman, an author on leadership skills and contributor to Forbes[4], says that it is the role of a manager to be "like a broken record" when it comes to establishing a vision for a team.

3. Build a team that is continuously learning

A highly effective team continues to learn and implement new skills over time. This can be done either through learning on the job, learning from colleagues, or it can be in the form of your company providing tools and resources to learn new skills.

As a manager, it is your role to notice skill gaps and encourage those on your team to take on new training, and/or experiences that would lessen these gaps. You can also regularly ask your team whether any new skills are needed, whether they personally have any desire to learn something that would benefit the group and to encourage those who may not feel ready that they can expand their skills. It will help the team as a whole!

4. Establish clear and measurable goals

Managers can help their teams create SMART goals which are easily understood and clear to follow. What are SMART goals? While this term has largely been adopted by businesses in general, a blog post by the Corporate Finance Institute[5] explains that it is a goal that is **S**pecific, **M**easurable, **A**chievable, **R**ealistic, and **T**imely.

The blog post lays out specific questions that should be asked for each of these areas. Consider the following questions as you are creating goals for your team:

Specific:

1. Who is involved in this goal?
2. What do I want to accomplish?
3. Where is this goal to be achieved?
4. When do I want to achieve this goal?
5. Why do I want to achieve this goal?

Measurable:

1. How many, how much?
2. How do I know if I have reached my goal?
3. What is my indicator of progress?

Achievable:

1. Do I have the resources and capabilities to achieve the goal? If not, what am I missing?
2. Have others done it successfully before?

Realistic:

1. Is the goal realistic and within reach?
2. Is the goal reachable, given the time and resources?
3. Are you able to commit to achieving the goal?

Timely:

1. Does my goal have a deadline?
2. By when do you want to achieve your goal?

Walking through each of these questions will help you define goals that are clear, and which motivate your team to achieve great things.

Motivating Managers

Motivating managers is slightly different from motivating a team. While it is common to consider what motivates employees generally, it can be easy to overlook the need to motivate your management team, as well. While every employee is responsible for certain roles and responsibilities, you'll specifically want to ensure that your management team is motivated so that they can bring out the best in all of your employees. Below is a list of items you can consider when thinking about what motivates managers specifically.

1. Challenging and Interesting Work

Challenging and interesting work may not be the first thing that comes to mind when you think of motivating managers, but a Harvard Business Review article[6] says we shouldn't overlook it. The author of the article, John Baldoni, quotes Fiona Dent, Director of Executive Education at U.K.'s Ashbridge Business School.

> *"Managers want to be treated as individuals. [T]here [needs] to be a clear understanding of what types of motivation work best to gain results from different individuals and teams."*

Managers, like other employees, want to be challenged and want to have interesting work. Make sure you do not overlook this as you think of ways to motivate your managers and those who manage people in your organization or company.

2. Compensation

Many people are motivated by a higher paycheck. If you have a manager who has this type of motivation, you can look to tie success into increased opportunities for bonuses for your managers. Make sure you align the incentives with the priorities of your business. Managers should be encouraged to pursue goals that help move the business forward and rewarded when they hit those goals.

3. Inclusion

There is another opportunity to motivate managers as you or higher-level executives are setting the strategy for an organization. When possible, you can seek the advice and feedback of managers as you are creating future plans for an organization.

Why would you want to include them? If you include them, they are more likely inclined to feel "bought-in." They will feel as though they are important to an organization and that their opinion matters. Many people simply want to feel valued and including managers in longer-term strategy and planning is one way to do this.

4. Acknowledgement

Sometimes an organization is so large that knowing what everyone is working on is simply not possible. In this case, middle managers can get lost in the crowd and feel as though their work is not important. Acknowledgement of work efforts, as well as successes, is one way to motivate managers. How can you do this?

- Share with your executive team your desire to promote acknowledgement and recognition throughout the organization. Solicit ideas on how you can do this (if you aren't doing it already).
- Establish a monthly or quarterly "win" get-together

where you celebrate the wins of departments and
organizations.

- Ask your managers to have one on one meetings with
  all direct reports so that they can more regularly
  acknowledge the efforts of their own employees and so
  that they can share those with higher levels of
  leadership.
- Acknowledge small things like birthdays or work start
  date anniversaries as a way to promote inclusion.

There may be many different ways that employees want to be
acknowledged and often, they can vary from individual to
individual. Continue to make this type of recognition a priority
and you will find many ways to celebrate those who work with
and for you.

5. Autonomy

As we mentioned earlier in the book, micromanaging is one of
the fastest ways to kill motivation among employees—especially
managers who are responsible for groups of people within an
organization. Autonomy can be a strong motivator for certain
individuals. Giving someone space to do their job (and not
dictating how it gets done), can allow managers to really "own"
a portion of the business, which can be very motivating!

Certain people don't want full autonomy. Perhaps they want
their leadership to check in on them regularly, or perhaps they
feel they need regular feedback in their job for a variety of

reasons. You can establish how often you will check in with your direct reports. It may surprise you how different the answers are depending on the manager! The best place to start is always to *ask* what someone's expectations and hopes are in terms of how much autonomy they want on a day-to-day basis.

Motivation Techniques

When it comes to motivating managers and employees there are a variety of ways you can go about it. Earlier we addressed motivating managers specifically but, in this section, we'll speak more broadly about the various ways that you can motivate employees and high-performing teams to make sure they are being coached to perform at the highest level possible.

Before we review the techniques themselves it is important to acknowledge that (generally), men and women are motivated by different things. IDG Research Services, along with Motivation Factor® and Boston Research Group, came out with an infographic[7] displaying the differences in motivation between men and women.

Women place higher importance on the following items in an organization:

- I need to have *balance* in my life.
- I need to feel *respected.*
- I often rely on my *intuition.*
- *Listening* to others' stories comes naturally to me.

- My *empathy* is an important resource to me.

Whereas men place importance on several different attributes:

- It is very important to me to *succeed* at what I set out to succeed.
- It is exciting to generate *new initiatives.*
- It is important to me to keep my *deadlines.*
- I must know the *truth.*
- It is important to me to attain my *goals.*

As you read through the following motivation techniques, keep these differences between men and women in mind so that you can tailor them to the needs of your team.

What are motivation techniques?

These techniques are different ways in which you can internally or externally motivate your employees. They should increase productivity and satisfaction overall at work. The techniques below are merely suggestions, and you will not see the results of them overnight. That takes time. You can also consider surveying your employees to see how each of them is motivated. Also, if promoting from within is important to you, you may consider training programs that help you build a pool of talent that allows you to plan for future leadership.

Technique #1: Set smaller, more easily achievable goals

If you have a large project that will take a lot of time to complete you may want to consider setting smaller goals throughout the project. This allows your team to stay motivated as they hit smaller milestones throughout, and also allows for course correction and feedback as pieces of the overall project are completed over time.

Technique #2: Create a culture of positivity

Happiness has been shown to positively affect productivity. Where possible, establish a culture of positivity, and encourage your leaders to do the same. Ask for employees with high levels of energy and naturally positive attitudes to contribute ideas on how to better incorporate this into the company culture.

Technique #3: Establish a mentorship program

As we mentioned earlier, high-performance teams should always be learning. A mentorship program is an easy way to pair more experienced and tenured employees with newer or less experienced employees. While these relationships should not be forced, they should provide the opportunity to build relationships over time, and, if structured correctly, can be a way for the mentee to learn new skills outside of their traditional job. This may motivate employees who are interested in learning and development opportunities as well as those who want stronger relationships throughout the organization.

Technique #4: Encourage a comfortable work environment

This includes acknowledging that employees should be taking breaks throughout the day to continually stay motivated. You may even want to consider offering amenities like fitness or meditation classes to your employees. Free snacks or lunch is another way to keep employee motivation high.

Technique #5: Offer profit-sharing (if possible)

If you are able and willing to share the profits of a company with employees, this is an excellent way to do so. This allows employees to have "ownership" in what happens in an organization and to realize the benefit when the company as a whole succeeds.

Technique #6: Additional benefits

There may be several other benefits that would motivate your employee base. Do they want more vacation days? A flexible schedule that allows them to work from home or remotely? You can easily find out what benefits employees desire by surveying them. You may not be able to implement them all but by using their input and implementing changes they will feel valued and heard.

In Summary

This chapter gave you a deep overview of what a high-performing team looks like, as well as how to motivate your managers and employees. Use these considerations and techniques as you create new teams or if you want to motivate current teams to be even more productive. Ultimately, if each member of a team is motivated and they all share a common goal, they will be unstoppable!

OVERCOMING SELF-DOUBT AND IMPOSTER SYNDROME

Self-doubt and imposter syndrome are two common stumbling blocks for successful women. The term "imposter syndrome" was first formally coined by two American psychologists, Pauline Clance and Suzanne Imes, in a 1978 study[1] focused on high-achieving women. In their study, Clance and Imes stated: "[D]espite outstanding academic and professional accomplishments, women who experience the imposter phenomenon persist in believing that they are really not bright and have fooled anyone who thinks otherwise."

The KPMG study we referenced earlier in Chapter 3 shared key findings related to imposter syndrome:

- As much as 75% of female executives report having personally experienced imposter syndrome at certain points in their career.
- Most of the survey respondents (85%) believe it is commonly experienced by women in corporate America.
- Seventy-four percent of executive women believe that their male counterparts do not experience feelings of self-doubt as much as female leaders do.
- Nearly half (47%) of executive women say that their feelings of imposter syndrome result from never expecting to reach the level of success they have achieved.

Recently, the global pandemic has increased imposter syndrome among certain groups of people. People who are scared of losing their jobs are more likely to experience imposter syndrome—and with good reason. Certain jobs have vanished, others have been restructured, and even more are now remote due to the current economy. Imposter syndrome may have someone working overtime and more visibly due to the fear (whether realistic or not) of being fired or let go.

If you want to be a high-performing female executive, it is important to recognize when self-doubt and imposter syndrome show up and equip yourself with ways to directly work through it. This chapter will also help you walk others through feelings of imposter syndrome and self-doubt; whether it is a peer or someone you are managing. Feeling like you are not good enough or that you don't belong is normal but knowing how to move past it is key. Let's look in depth at self-doubt and imposter syndrome. We'll also provide practical ways to approach both of them in your life.

What is Self-Doubt?

Professor Adam Grant at the University of Pennsylvania says in his book *Originals: How Non-Conformists Move the World,* that there are two kinds of doubt: self-doubt and idea doubt. Self-doubt is all about you . . . doubting your own abilities. Idea doubt is what encourages you to refine and test an idea. When you start to feel self-doubt, take the focus off of you and turn it into idea doubt. Perhaps what you're working on has never been done before. It doesn't say anything about *you*; feel free to tweak and adjust and refine over time. It's the idea that needs to be fleshed out, it's not a statement about your abilities. When possible, Professor Grant suggests we turn self-doubt into idea doubt to make progress over time.

What is Imposter Syndrome?

Imposter syndrome is a way of thinking that downplays our skills and makes us feel like a fraud. As though we don't belong and do not deserve to be where we are. It often forces you to focus on what could go wrong, how you (in your own mind) are not capable, and it makes you believe that at any moment you could be exposed—by a boss, colleague, or otherwise.

The 2020 KPMG Study on Women's Leadership (also referenced in Chapter 3) states that imposter syndrome is a "persistent inability to believe one's success is deserved or achieved by working hard and possessing distinct skills and capabilities but by other means such as luck or being at the right place at the right time. It is often accompanied with feelings of self-doubt, fear of success or failure, or self-sabotage."

Women and Imposter Syndrome

Imposter syndrome seems to affect women more than men. In fact, a 2011 study published in the *Journal of Economic Behavior & Organization* and Columbia Business School's *Ideas at Work* says that men are more confident than women and that is why there is a lack of women in the C-suite.[1] Not sure if you've ever felt imposter syndrome? Below is a list of common feelings associated with imposter syndrome:

- **You feel like at any moment you could be "found out" for not belonging**: You logically think that you belong but emotionally you don't feel that way. You are scared of being revealed as not really worthy.
- **You devalue yourself**: You don't understand why

people would want to pay you for your skills. You undersell yourself.

- **You play down your skills on purpose**: Instead of being proud of your experiences and skills that you can bring to a team and organization, you play it off as though you're not qualified enough. It's beyond humble; you diminish yourself in the eyes of others.

Famous women feel imposter syndrome too. They do! Read these quotes from extremely accomplished and well-known women. Do you recognize yourself in any of them?

"The greatest obstacle for me has been the voice in my head which I call my obnoxious roommate. I wish someone would invent a tape recorder that we could attach to our brains to record everything we tell ourselves. We would realize how important it is to stop this negative self-talk. It means pushing back against our obnoxious roommate with a dose of wisdom."

— ARIANNA HUFFINGTON

"I have written 11 books, but each time I think, 'uh oh, they're going to find out now. I've run a game on everybody and they're going to find me out.'"

— MAYA ANGELOU

"I still sometimes feel like a loser kid in high school and I just have to pick myself up and tell myself that I'm a superstar every morning so that I can get through this day and be for my fans what they need me to be."

— LADY GAGA

"I have spent my years since Princeton, while at law school and in my various professional jobs, not feeling completely a part of the worlds I inhabit. I am always looking over my shoulder wondering if I measure up."

— SONIA SOTOMAYOR

"Now when I receive recognition for my acting, I feel incredibly uncomfortable. I tend to turn in on myself. I feel like an imposter."

"Any moment, someone's going to find out I'm a total fraud, and that I don't deserve any of what I've achieved."

— EMMA WATSON

"I still have a little impostor syndrome... It doesn't go away, that feeling that you shouldn't take me that seriously. What do I know? I share that with you because we all have doubts in our abilities, about our power and what that power is."

— MICHELLE OBAMA

Very famous and accomplished people also feel like they may not belong. No one is immune! Remember this the next time you feel out of place; you're in good company.

A Quick History on Women, the Workplace, and Imposter Syndrome

A Harvard Business Review article titled *Stop Telling Women They Have Imposter Syndrome,*[3] rightfully points out that "the impact of systemic racism, classism, xenophobia, and other biases was categorically absent when the concept of imposter syndrome was developed. Many groups were excluded from the study, namely women of color and people of various income levels, genders, and professional backgrounds. Even as we know it today, imposter syndrome puts the blame on individuals, without accounting for the historical and cultural contexts that are foundational to how it manifests in both women of color and white women. Imposter syndrome directs our view toward fixing women at work instead of fixing the places where women work."

It is interesting to consider that women were often "categorized" with imposter syndrome, or labelling it as something to be fixed, rather than acknowledging *why* imposter syndrome may be prevalent, specifically for women, in the first place.

How Employers and Managers can Tackle Imposter Syndrome in Employees

If you or other employees are regularly feeling imposter syndrome, there are some things that an organization or company can do to address the issue head-on. The same

Harvard Business Review article above states: "The answer to overcoming imposter syndrome is not to fix individuals but to create an environment that fosters a variety of leadership styles and in which diverse racial, ethnic, and gender identities are seen as just as professional as the current model..."

Also, it is important to realize the effect that imposter syndrome can have on women of colour, who often face discrimination on several levels: for being a woman, a woman of colour, and dealing with any unconscious bias from others. For women of colour specifically, feelings of doubt and imposter syndrome come from years of systemic bias and racism and multiple layers of bias and stereotypes applied and directed towards them over time.

The KPMG Women's Leadership Report shares two key items that survey respondents said could mitigate imposter syndrome in the workplace:

1. Having a supportive performance manager (47% of respondents) was the primary workplace factor to help reduce feelings of imposter syndrome.
2. Feeling valued and being rewarded fairly (29% of respondents).

Where possible, create a work environment that is inclusive and diverse, allowing for different work and leadership styles. This will show people, and specifically women and women of colour, that what makes them different and unique is not only needed but welcomed and honoured.

Self-Doubt and Imposter Syndrome

The KPMG Women's Leadership Report states that the "first step in overcoming Imposter Syndrome is recognizing the signs and acknowledging the feelings." According to an article titled *The Confidence Gap*[4] in The Atlantic, "[women] have made undeniable progress. In the United States, women now earn more college and graduate degrees than men do. We make up half the workforce, and we are closing the gap in middle management...And yet, as we've worked, ever diligent, the men around us have continued to get promoted faster and be paid more. The statistics are well known: at the top, especially, women are nearly absent, and our numbers are barely increasing. Half a century since women first forced open the boardroom doors, our career trajectories still look very different from men's."

This section of the chapter will offer different techniques for dealing with self-doubt and imposter syndrome. Now that you can recognize what self-doubt and imposter syndrome look like these techniques should help you move through the fears that cause you to freeze up or hold still.

Take action

Taking action, even when you do not feel entirely confident, can help you overcome self-doubt and imposter syndrome. It shows the world that you are willing to try and potentially, fail. But you could also succeed, which will build confidence in your skills.

Whenever possible, do not let self-doubt or imposter syndrome paralyze you. Make a plan of action and take it one step at a time to break through any fear you may be feeling.

Make an "accomplishments" list

Chances are you have accomplished a lot of things. Perhaps you're so focused on how you do not belong that you might be overlooking them! When imposter syndrome strikes make a quick list of things that you *have* done. Things you have already accomplished. This will take your focus off perceived threats and will (hopefully) help you to feel slightly more grounded in reality and aware of the things you've done in the past.

Speak positively to yourself

Research has shown that positive self-talk works! A study[5] by psychologist Ethan Kross of the University of Michigan showed that how you speak to yourself actually does matter. "What we find," Kross says, "is that a subtle linguistic shift — shifting from 'I' to your own name — can have really powerful self-regulatory effects." Instead of saying "I am confident," it would be more powerful and impactful to insert your name: "Jemma is confident." Try this technique to build up your self-esteem when you notice self-doubt rising.

Lower your expectations

Often, women experience imposter syndrome because they expect perfection when others are merely expecting "good enough." Many women think perfection is what is required when it is merely their own expectation that places so much pressure on ourselves. "Smart women often see perfection as a synonym for achievement," says Carol Dweck, Ph.D., a Stanford University psychologist and author of *Mindset: The New Psychology of Success*. The minute we start to struggle, we think, Oops, maybe I don't belong here." Dweck says not to undervalue your efforts. Working hard doesn't mean that you're not *good* at something; it means you're developing your skills, something every great leader should be doing.

In a Forbes article titled *The Confidence Gap: Six Ways Women Can Dismantle the Hurdles in Their Own Heads,* Dr. Margie Warrell writes: "We get stuck on a perfectionist merry-go-round, of striving but never arriving, when we buy into the misguided belief that we must be absolutely masterful at a skill or know 100% exactly what we're doing before we take the first step. Then when we do step out and our efforts don't land in a perfect 10, we use our fallen moments as a baton to flog ourselves with. Little wonder so many women are perpetually exhausted."

Sound familiar? Dr. Warrell argues that when we lower our expectations (of ourselves and others) we free up time to diversify what we work and focus on, leading to more balanced lives overall.

Replace 'shoulds' with 'coulds'

Perhaps you need a change in perspective. Many times, we grow up with social and societal norms of what our work and personal lives "should" look like. In the same Forbes article mentioned above, Dr. Warrell argues that we should replace every one of these "shoulds" with "coulds." So, *should* you go to bed by 9 pm? Or *could* you? What a difference a word makes. Replacing the 'shoulds' in your life with 'coulds' reminds you that only you get to live your life and you have the freedom to make many of the choices that affect how you go throughout your day.

Lean on your fellow women

The KPMG Women's Leadership Report rightfully points out that "communication and collaboration play a vital role in helping to reduce self-doubt and promote self-worth." If you have a boss that is supportive of you in your role and who believes in the impact you can have then you'll be less likely to stay with a feeling of imposter syndrome for long. Alternatively, if you are in a position of managing others, be sure to encourage and affirm them regularly. Check in to see how they are doing and, where possible, ensure that they feel comfortable, secure, and valued.

Women tend to compare and compete more with women than with other men. However, when women succeed, they tend to bring up other women under them as well. What does this mean? It means that there is power in the collective. If you are a woman who has only a handful of other women in your workplace, work to befriend them, not to compete with them. You all should not be "tokens," but rather, can harness your unique and diverse capabilities to more positively impact your organization.

Don't wait to feel comfortable

If you're waiting for the perfect time to do something . . . for the right amount of confidence, for the perfect situation to appear, you may be waiting for a long time. The reality is that *most* people feel fear when they are not totally comfortable. But those who succeed do so because they push through it. If fear is totally debilitating remember to take a deep breath. Acknowledge your feelings and honour them, because they are real. However, give yourself positive self-talk and remind yourself that everyone feels fear and that it's ok not to be perfect. Take it one step at a time but no matter what, keep moving forward.

Silence your inner critic

We all have one . . . that nagging voice inside of you that tells you that you're not good enough, not perfect enough . . . never "enough." As you watch your thoughts notice that you don't have to *believe* or *buy into* them. There are various ways that you can do this:

- Acknowledge that your critic is not you. It's simply a voice in your head that is reacting to fear.
- Don't pay attention to the competition. Focus your eyes and efforts on the end goal and not on what others are doing.
- Admit that you don't know it all! Nobody knows everything about every topic. It's ok to say that you need time to find the answer. I guarantee that people will respect you for admitting that you want to take the time to get them the *right* answer rather than simply coming up with a fast answer.
- Find an ally. Do you have someone who can support and encourage you when needed? Someone you can lean on and who can help you silence your inner critic? Tell you how it *actually* is, rather than how you're perceiving it? Could you also be someone else's ally?

Tips for Leaders

I'd like to close this chapter with a few things to keep in mind if you lead a team or happen to be in a position of leadership within an organization. If you are in a role like this, you have immense opportunity to lead by example and affect the culture of a group or part of an organization. Pulled from the KPMG Women's Leadership Report, here are five ways you can establish a culture that fights against self-doubt and imposter syndrome:

Be Supportive

We've discussed the need to manage people individually and this is one area you can do so. Each person has different needs in a work environment and through regular interaction, you'll notice if someone needs a little encouragement. Create an environment in which it is ok to try, and it is especially ok to fail. If anything, failing means you have simply found one way that does not work. Build your team up and instil confidence in them.

Promote a Collaborative Culture

People who feel as though they are part of a team are less likely to doubt themselves for long. Why? Because other team members will encourage them and help them as they stumble. Encourage your team to check in on and help one another. Welcome empathy and kindness into your culture and as much as possible, encourage everyone to work as a team to get projects done.

Promote Inclusion and Diversity

We've already discussed how valuable diversity is to high-performance teams. Inclusion and diversity also help banish self-doubt since people will know that what makes them unique and different is valued and that they will not be forced to change themselves to fit in. Show everyone constantly that they are valued and that they need to and should feel comfortable contributing in only the way that they can; the team needs it to be as effective as possible!

Value Progress

While it's common to work towards goals and deadlines, value progress, and celebrate "small wins" along the way. This will help build your team's confidence over time. The KPMG report suggests even having incentives that celebrate incremental progress and "not just end results." This also allows you to address any issues of self-doubt or lack of confidence that may come up along the way.

Encourage Work/Life Balance

Encouraging a work/life balance will not only prevent burnout but will show your employees that you care about their lives—both in and outside of work. Respect any time off that your employees may take and have a genuine interest in getting to know how your employees spend their time away from work.

In Summary

Everyone, even extremely accomplished people, is likely to feel self-doubt and imposter syndrome. Now that you have a good idea of what self-doubt and imposter syndrome look like it will be easier to spot in your life and the lives of others.

Whenever you notice it, remember that this isn't something

you alone are experiencing. This has been felt by many others, and specifically many women before you. Try some of the tactics suggested to tackle it as it appears and choose to look at it as a positive: experiencing these things likely means that you are stretching your skills and pushing yourself outside of your comfort zone. Remind yourself that you belong, you have lots to contribute, and that you deserve to be here . . . because you do!

BUILDING SELF-CONFIDENCE IN YOU AND YOUR TEAM

If you notice that someone (either someone on your team or you, yourself) has self-doubt or is experiencing imposter syndrome then you have a huge opportunity. It is likely that once you've tackled the fear of not belonging you recognize that there are deeper, more significant self-confidence issues that are contributing to this self-doubt.

This chapter addresses the mental barriers you or others may face related to self-confidence. Having high levels of self-confidence will help a good team become even more effective, and will put your team on track to becoming a "high-performance team."

Women and Self-Confidence

The Merriam-Webster dictionary defines confidence as "a feeling or consciousness of one's powers or of reliance on one's circumstances." Aimee Cohen, a Denver, Colorado-based career coach and author says, "It requires really paying attention to the small wins and not being so quick to overlook, downplay, dismiss and diminish your accomplishments."

Women are less likely than men to enter the workforce and believe they can climb the corporate ladder. According to a Bain and LinkedIn survey[1] of 8,400 adults, 63% of women, compared with 75% of men, enter the workforce with the belief that they can rise to senior management. By mid-career, the stats were even worse with 57% of women believing they could rise to the top of senior management compared with 66% of men in the same position.

Journalists Katty Kay and Claire Shipman published *The Confidence Code* in 2014. After years of covering high-profile women, Kay and Shipman realized that almost everyone dealt with self-doubt. In a *Times* article[2] reviewing the book, Jessica Bennett stated, "In two decades covering American politics, the two journalists had interviewed some of the most powerful women in the nation — lawmakers and CEOs, professional athletes, leaders of social movements. Time and again, they saw the same self-doubt: bright women with ideas afraid to raise their hands, speak up, ask for a raise or a promotion; that inexplicable feeling that they don't *own the right* to rule at the top."

So what does a lack of self-confidence look like? Bennett writes that it could be any of the following:

- "When a professional endeavour goes wrong, women are more likely to blame themselves. Yet when something goes right, they credit circumstance – or other people – for their success. (Men do the opposite.)"

- "Women are more likely than men to be perfectionists, holding themselves back from answering a question, applying for a new job, asking for a raise, until they're *absolutely 100 percent sure* we can predict the outcome. (Women applied for a promotion only when they met 100 percent of the qualifications. Men applied when they met 50 percent.)"

- "Women are a quarter as likely as men to negotiate a raise. We doubt our opinions and begin our sentences with "I don't know if this is right, but—." We are more prone to "rumination" than men – which causes us to overthink and overanalyze. (Sound familiar?)"

Recognizing that these feelings exist is the first step. Building your self-confidence does take time and there is not only one right way to do it. But recognizing that this feeling isn't *you* . . .

can be reassuring as you work to build your self-confidence over time.

Ways to build self-confidence

There are many effective ways to build and support the growth of self-confidence over time. Here are three ideas that you may want to try:

1. Starting a confidence log or journal

The key to changing anything is awareness. Start to keep track of times when you feel confident or where you lack self-confidence. This requires attention, presence, and awareness in the moment. You may also find surprising things as a result of this. Perhaps there are certain situations or people around which you find you have less self-confidence. Here are a few examples of how you might tackle this:

- You notice that you lack self-confidence around presentations. So, you ask a trusted mentor to provide feedback and you practise many times alone before having to give a formal presentation. After each subsequent presentation, you notice if you felt more or less confident (hopefully more!) and you see what else you can practise or tweak to continue to build your skills over time.

- A higher-level executive makes you extremely nervous. You discuss this with your boss and find that this is not limited to just you—they make everyone feel that way. Your boss helps you prepare in advance for meetings with this executive and helps you work through any worries or potential questions you may have. Your confidence grows as you understand that you have allies and that this executive's behaviour is not personal towards you.

Keeping a confidence log or journal may be very eye-opening for you. Try it out for a week or more and see how it goes. If it's helpful, continue the practice.

2. Start a "brag book" or "happy folder"

Anytime someone sends a 'thank you' note, an encouraging note, or notices something that you do extremely well, consider saving it to a physical 'brag book' or digital 'happy folder.' This should be a collection of moments where you have gone above and beyond and where it has been obviously noticed by others.

The magic of a 'brag book' or 'happy folder' is when things *aren't* going as well as you had hoped. In those times, you can flip through (or browse) and remember when others recognized you as kind, thoughtful, strong, courageous, helpful, etc. You may at first feel silly to start keeping these items. But if you're ever in a position to need an emotional 'pick-me-up' you will be surprised how poignant and encouraging these items can be. Why? Because they are real. They are real notes and items from a past time when you were a great help to someone else. And ultimately, that will make you feel really good (and rightfully so!).

3. Sit at the table, and speak up

Many women are invited to meetings but feel they shouldn't "sit at the table." Instead, they choose a spot around the outer edge of the room, under the guise of being "respectful." There is something positive to be said for respect. It's important to be humble in a leadership position and to have respect for those whom you work with and for. However, don't diminish yourself self worth!

If you're invited, feel free to sit at the table if there is room. Speak up when you have something meaningful to add to the conversation. Remember that you are here for a reason, and you were invited to the meeting for a reason. You don't need to hog all of the attention, nor should you feel compelled to have a comment for every item on the agenda. But where possible, speak up and contribute. Your organization will appreciate this as there are only things that *you*, in your unique background and capacity, can add.

How to Convey Confidence

Noah Zandan, CEO and Co-Founder of Quantified Communications, an Austin, TX communications-analytics firm, says that first impressions are formed within 15–20 seconds of meeting someone. Even if you spend a significant amount of time with someone, 90% of the time their original opinions of you remain unchanged. This is significant! If your first impression is formed within the first minute or so of meeting someone, you'll want to be aware of some simple ways to convey confidence even when you do not "feel" confident. Consider doing one or more of the below items to display your confidence and build it over time:

- **Maintain eye contact**: A lack of direct eye contact may mean a lack of confidence. So, eye contact *can* convey confidence. Don't overdo it, though! Nobody likes to be stared down.

- **Stand still:** When speaking to someone else don't constantly shift your weight back and forth or stand only on one foot which can show nervousness. Firmly plant your feet to the ground and *feel* firm and strong in your stance.

- **Stand tall:** In addition to standing still, you'll also want to stand tall. What does this mean? Back straight, chin up, shoulders down and legs hip width apart.

- **Be natural and authentic:** Make sure that whatever you are doing, especially if it is not natural to you, does not come across as fake. The last thing you want to do is distract someone you are speaking with due to an abnormal posture, shifting of your weight, or being too rigid. If you're really nervous just remember to breathe and be yourself.

Small but Impactful Ways to Build Confidence

Women are less likely to speak up for themselves and ask for what they need and want. However, there are things you can do to grow your confidence in this area over time.

Ask for small things

According to research from Linda Babcock at Carnegie Mellon,[3] women are "four times less likely to ask for a raise, and also are more likely to underestimate their abilities at work." While most women may not be comfortable asking for a promotion or a raise right away, perhaps there are other things that you *can* ask for: the ability to flex your work hours during the day, or perhaps to split your time between the office and home throughout the workweek. As result of the Covid-19 pandemic, offices have adapted so that more are able to work from home. We have proven that we can work efficiently from home, which is a huge step for women wanting to have a better work/life family balance. This may mean more women in power are less likely to step-down from their careers.

Asking for small things does three things that help you to build confidence:

1. It allows you to acknowledge your needs.
2. It requires you to articulate these out loud to others who can actually do something about them.
3. It may positively change your life!

The worst thing that could happen from an ask like this is that someone says 'no.'

Ok . . . then, you are right back where you started. But now, you have learned that you *can* ask for things you need and want, and you have strengthened your confidence muscle in doing so!

List out your positive attributes

For many of us, we can list out the positive attributes of others in a split second. If asked what the most positive traits of a colleague are we don't bat an eyelid. We're able to list them *all* out, and explain why. When it comes to ourselves, however, we may be at a loss. Why is that?

Sometimes it's hard to see ourselves objectively. Instead of acknowledging our skills, we might think a task is so easy a monkey could do it. Instead of admitting our obvious expertise due to prior job experience, we may say that it was "luck."

To combat this, take out a sheet of paper and list out some recent accomplishments. Also, list out what you consider to be your positive attributes. Once you stop writing or once it comes to a pause, push yourself to write even more. Why? Because acknowledging your positive traits, having self-confidence and self-respect will allow you to see these qualities in others, too.

Ways Women can Display more Self-Confidence at Work

Mel Robbins, an American lawyer, television host, author, and motivational speaker, has described confidence as not a state, but rather, a feeling. She says, "It's a skill, one that must be built through repeated acts of everyday courage." Robbins says that low levels of confidence "breeds hesitation and inaction, but if you force yourself to actually take action, you'll do better than you even thought you could–which actually builds confidence and makes you perform even better." Robbins recommends seven ways[4] that women can build more self-confidence at work:

1. Tap into the Progress Principle

The Progress Principle was created by Harvard researcher Teresa Amabile. The idea is that "celebrating small wins" is the most important thing when it comes to creating a positive work-life. How do you celebrate small wins? You can make a list of them as they occur throughout the day. Robbins also points out that this list of wins can be very useful when it comes time to discuss your contribution to your team, when you're asking for a raise or a promotion, or when a formal review time comes up. You'll have a built-in list of accomplishments and wins ready to discuss with your manager.

2. Manage Your Visibility

Robbins argues that the "#1 thing you can do to display your confidence at work is to be more visible." An easy way to do this is to speak up in meetings. If you often get nervous about contributing in meetings there are some things you can do to get yourself comfortable ahead of time:

- If you are unfamiliar with the topic of the meeting, prepare yourself ahead of time. If you need information or further context, ask the organizer of the meeting for anything that might help you prep.
- Before the meeting, think of questions you have or items you may be able to contribute.
- Psych yourself up! Speak confidently and kindly to yourself. Encourage yourself to contribute using your full name as we learned in Chapter 5.

3. Be a Strategic Contributor

Generally, in a strong and aligned organization, the goals of a team all build upon one another. For example, if your goal is to bring $100,000 in new revenue to the organization, then your boss's goal might be to bring in $500,000 as a team, and the department head's goal might be even larger than that.

Unfortunately, most organizations are not structured in this way. What does that mean for you? It means that you should be very particular about which projects you take on and that you should want them to align with your boss' and team's priorities. When you do this, you are ensuring that your efforts are positively impacting your team and organization and that you're not just working on things *you* want to work on that are not for the greater good of the team.

4. Solve Problems

We've discussed a lot throughout this book about how strong female leaders see issues and resolve them. If they can't solve them by themselves, they do the very best they can and they bring potential solutions.

As a leader, it is your role to resolve issues you see as they arise. Robbins encourages us not to let perfectionism stop us from tackling a problem. The solution doesn't have to be perfect, and it doesn't have to be resolved immediately.

You can also empower your team, and specifically females on your team to do the same. When everyone starts solving problems immediately the team is more effective and able to focus on the issues as a group that require collaboration to be resolved.

5. Send a Failure Post-Mortem

Robbins writes about a practice at Etsy that involves acknowledging failures publicly after they occur:

> *"At Etsy, people are encouraged to document their mistakes and how the mistakes happened–in public emails! A "post-mortem" (means "post-death") is a practice that's used at Etsy. If something goes wrong, the entire team has a post-mortem and tries to "find out what went wrong and make it better, not to blame." The company has found this practice*

> *encourages innovation and risk-taking because people*
> *don't feel afraid to make a mistake."*

Perhaps your company culture is (whether via email or in a meeting) to acknowledge when things did not go according to plan you'd want to establish that it is a safe space for discussion and collaboration and that the goal would be to collectively determine what went wrong and how it can be prevented in the future. Where possible, lead by example and build it into any team meetings that you might manage. Over time, it may become part of your team's culture and potentially even that of your larger organization.

6. Say No

Most people, especially women, view the word 'no' as a negative statement. By saying you cannot do something you may fear that you are letting someone down and hurting someone else's feelings or people may think you do not have the ability to do the task . But saying 'no' to things that are not a current priority is a boundary. It allows you to protect those things that your job requires of you: the things which pay your bills, and which are promotable opportunities. When you are offered something that does not fall on that list and which would take time away from what's been entrusted only to you, you can confidently say 'no,' because it frees you up to do more of what you were originally hired to do.

Robbins rightly points out that it does depend on where the request comes from. If it's from someone outside your team and you feel you need to decline, you may want to help them find another person who can help support the project. If, however, your boss asks you to take something on that was not originally labelled as a priority see it as an opportunity to have a discussion on what's important *now* to the team. Maybe, it's that your priorities have changed or perhaps they need to shift based on new business initiatives or needs. The important thing is to always be clear on what you're expected to do and to confidently say 'no' to everything that may take time away from what's most important.

7. Set Boundaries

Even when women work in an office, they stereotypically still take on a majority of household duties as well. This means that working women can be more subject to burnout over the long run than their male counterparts. How do you avoid burnout? By setting clear boundaries.

Here are five ways to set boundaries on your time and expectations:

- Be honest and confident about your work hours and when you will be "on" with other colleagues.
- When you are "off" (i.e., when it's outside of work hours), *relax*. Don't answer emails. Consistently stick

to the boundaries that you have set and train others to do the same.

- Don't check in via email or phone during unexpected times like weekends and outside of work hours.

- Treat the boundaries of others as you would expect yours to be treated; don't "catch up" on emails and send a flurry to subordinates or colleagues outside of work hours just to empty out your inbox and therefore put the next steps on them. If they report to you, they will especially feel pressure to check in and respond, no matter what time your note was sent.

- Recognize that imposter syndrome has made people work harder and even more than they normally would. Where possible, encourage your team to have a work-life balance and show them that you value this by also implementing it in your own life.

In Summary

While confidence is often viewed as a skill that you either have or do not have, it is possible to strengthen your confidence muscle over time. In times of difficulty, lean on people who know and love you, and who can speak truth and encouragement into your life.

Take baby steps . . . do small, incremental things that build confidence, one at a time. And then, progressively take on bigger risks where appropriate. Ask yourself: "What's the worst that could happen?" Usually, the "worst possible scenario" is something that we've built up in our heads, but which doesn't really exist in real life. And usually, even when something doesn't work out perfectly, we will likely have an opportunity to try again. If needed, slow down or pause. But don't quit!

COMMUNICATION SECRETS OF THE MOST SUCCESSFUL WOMEN

Communication is not just a skill that is needed in the workplace. Wherever you have relationships, be it romantic, familial, or in the office, communication skills are necessary. Strong communication skills can enhance relationships and build trust over time. This chapter will explain how men and women differ in communication, how to start building stronger communication skills, and tips to consider as you work on building your communication skills in an office environment.

How Men and Women Differ in Communication

There is no way to avoid it: men and women tend to communicate differently. A study[1] from Catalyst, a New York nonprofit focused on helping women in business, found that 81% of women say that adopting a communications style that makes men feel comfortable was key to advancing their careers. This shows how important it is to be able to communicate effectively with the opposite gender and the potential impact it can have on a female executive's career trajectory.

One major difference in communication styles is pointed out by Sandra Beckwith, author of *Why Can't a Man Be More Like a Woman?* Beckwith states that a large difference between men and women is in how they gather information. Women gather information by asking questions where men view questions as weakness.

There are many other ways that men and women differ in communicating. Here are some examples of those differences:

- Women are seen as more collaborative whereas men are more competitive and assertive.
- Women tend to speak in higher and softer pitched voices. Men in lower and louder voices.
- Women ask questions and men do not.
- Women tend to want to be liked and to fit in while men want to stand out.
- Women desire to focus on relationships whereas men focus on power.
- Women speak to collect information and men speak to give information.
- Women tend to speak about relationships and men will speak about things.

- Women tend to intuit and feel and men focus on facts and logic.

Cultural differences can also contribute to how men and women communicate. In some societies, women are raised to be "nice," which can affect how they interact and communicate with others. All of these things are important to keep in mind and to be aware of, especially if you have a team composed of both men and women.

In today's digital world, remote meetings can make it even harder for women to be heard among male colleagues. A study by Yale psychologist Victoria Brescoll[2] found that male executives who spoke more often are often viewed as more competent, whereas if a female executive did the same thing, she was deemed less competent.

According to Deborah Tannen, professor of linguistics at Georgetown University who studies how men and women speak, any communication imbalances, such as men speaking over women or taking credit for their ideas, are amplified online in virtual meetings. Tannen states that imbalances in communication can be boiled down to differences in communication styles and conventions. These differences often include an imbalance in speaking time, length of time between speakers, frequency of questions received, and amount of conversations happening at the same time (i.e., overlapping discussions). While teaching classes online, Tannen discovered that although she thought remote learning would encourage those who were shy to speak up, it actually had an inverse effect. Those who were reticent to speak in person were even more so once they entered a virtual classroom. We would likely expect to see the same for digital meetings in the workplace, especially as women are often less likely to speak up in person. It can also be difficult to read body language and understand nonverbal cues while in a digital meeting, so it's important to look out for these cues to better enhance communication— especially when you are in a digital meeting. It may also help you encourage certain people who may be hesitant to contribute to speak up.

Noticing the differences in how men and women communicate is the first step towards understanding how to communicate with the other gender in the workplace. This skill is necessary for any successful female executive as she climbs the corporate ladder.

How to Build These Skills

If you have a desire to build your communication skills the first thing to keep in mind is that it requires *awareness*. Much of how we communicate today is the result of many things: our upbringing, conscious or unconscious beliefs, and even spoken and unspoken expectations (from ourselves or others).

Before making any changes, it is important to become aware of how you speak at work. There are some different ways to do this:

- Ask a colleague to listen carefully to you in a meeting and for their feedback afterwards.
- Have a meeting with your boss or team and gather feedback on how you communicate.
- If you are recorded for any reason, be it a presentation or call, listen to it again to hear how you speak and communicate in more formal settings.

What you want to determine is whether your communication style and strategy are working for you. Once you start to pay attention to how you are communicating you can start to ask yourself whether it's authentic to who you are, whether others understand you often and clearly, and whether there is anything you can do to build and enhance your skills.

Once you have thought through the above items, you may decide that you need some new communication skills to help prepare you for the next stage of your career. It takes practice to build new skills. You can take advantage of networking events to practise newly learned skills. Or, you can ask someone you trust to be your accountability partner. They can encourage you to practice throughout the week and then you can check in weekly to see how you're making progress.

There are many ways to go about building new skills but the important place to start is to recognize where you are and to measure the impact of your current communication habits and techniques.

Common Communication Pitfalls

Lois P. Frankel, author of *Nice Women Don't Get the Corner Office,* says that there are common things that women do through communication that undermine their influence and authority. These include:

- Using too many words to deliver serious messages.
- Not acknowledging or downplaying their contribution.
- Qualifying their opinions to lessen their authority.
- Using vague language.
- Forming a sentence as a question rather than a statement.
- Ending a sentence on an upward inflection or pitch, which can show signs of doubt.
- Not speaking confidently enough.
- Leading with emotions and feelings rather than facts and reason.
- Not being concise in your communications.
- Taking up too little space (e.g., sitting on the edge of the room rather than the table or speaking too infrequently).

Being aware of common pitfalls will help you to focus on which communication skills you may want to work on to increase your authority and influence. Next, we'll discuss general tips that convey confidence and will help you demonstrate authority when you communicate.

General Communication Tips

While this chapter applies to both men and women (everyone can benefit from strong communication!), we will address general communication tips that help combat typical stereotypes that women face every day in the workplace.

Speak confidently

Did you know that you can convey authority simply in the way that you speak? One way to do this is to speak with confidence, even when you are not feeling confident. How can you do this? One way is to lower your pitch. Often, men command attention and authority simply because they have louder and deeper voices. Unfortunately, sometimes women's voices are lost in meetings simply because they are in a higher pitch or range. Where possible (and when comfortable for you!) lower your pitch to speak in a slightly deeper tone to command attention confidently. A second way is to speak from your diaphragm. Singers do this to project their voices across a room. Speak more authoritatively by activating your core and speaking from your gut or stomach. Thirdly, don't be afraid to speak slower or to pause to add emphasis. This will command attention, especially if someone is expecting you to fly through a point and you take time to pause or speak with emphasis.

The Incedo Group, an organizational development consulting firm, says that three traits are crucial to effective communication for female executives: 1) credibility, 2) likeability, and 3) authority. All three of these can be communicated through confident speaking.

Communicate with facts and reason

One of the amazing things about women is that stereotypically, we can connect quickly with others through emotion. We are "feelers." However, when you want to have strong communication skills in the workplace, it is often a better tactic to stick to facts, logic, and reason when you are speaking.

Sticking to facts and reason (objective statements) focuses on important matters rather than your personal feelings about them. Ideally, it prevents you from straying off-topic or getting too impassioned while speaking. It is great to care about what you are saying. It may also be effective to stress how important something is to you. As a female, however, we often face the stereotype that women are emotional. One way to combat this is to stick to things that are not: objective facts, logic, and reason.

How do you do this? When you are relaying the information, stick to the facts and data rather than adding additional commentary or storytelling. You may also want to consider avoiding using the term "I feel" to describe any points you want to make. If you do say "I feel that . . ." others (unfortunately) may perceive this as a weakness.

Remove the "ums," "likes," and "ands"

Have you ever noticed when, um, someone says, um, filler words, in, like, every part of their sentence? It's distracting, right? If this is something that you normally do, practise speaking without filler words out loud. Filler words, if used every now and then, might not be distracting, but when used often they diminish your authority and could potentially lose the focus of or unintentionally distract those you are speaking to. Kelly Decker of Decker Communications says that pausing[3] can make all the difference in removing these filler words. If filler words are something that you use regularly practise speaking out loud and pausing strategically where you would normally place a filler word.

Do not be afraid to take up space

Women stereotypically make themselves smaller to fit in. However, to command authority and influence you may want to consider taking up more space. You may use certain gestures that help emphasize what you are saying or may also physically take up a larger space on a conference room table. This is also something to consider if you are presenting while standing. It is very easy to make a larger gesture which not only emphasizes what you are presenting but commands attention and authority.

Be as direct as possible

Women generally like to give as much background as possible when speaking. In addition, most women say that they don't like to be direct because they are afraid of hurting someone else's feelings. However, being direct will help you command respect as others start to learn that you mean what you say and will share what you think. You also don't need to justify every point that you want to make. Most women, when wanting to make a point will also include the background information, key findings, *why* they think it's important and potentially also caution the ideas as something that is "in their opinion." However, when you are confident in what you are saying, and if you want to command respect, do just that. Be direct and confident. Get straight to the point, and never apologize for doing so.

Some men believe that questions are a sign of weakness. One technique that works with men is changing any questions you may have into a statement. Instead of "What do you think about the project deadline?" you may say, "Tell me your thoughts on the deadline." This is simple and direct. As a communications technique, it will resonate with many people but especially men.

Being direct and getting straight to the point prevents you from including anecdotes which could confuse listeners and prevent people from losing interest. You may also unknowingly "water down" your message with things that are not as important if you stray at all from the point you are trying to make.

Being direct is also incredibly helpful when you are having hard conversations. Nobody enjoys these, and under these circumstances, brevity and directness will be even more appreciated. If you have to deliver a hard message, provide a colleague with undesirable feedback or are simply having a challenging conversation try being as succinct as possible in your message. It will be appreciated on both sides.

Be focused

Try not to be scattered in presenting your points, thoughts, or opinions in a meeting. The easier it is to understand what you are saying the more likely others are to respect what you bring to the table. Ask yourself: what one or two key ideas do I want to convey? What is most important? Once you determine these points, stick to them as best as you can.

Connect with others

Women, more so than men, can be empathetic and know how to make genuine connections with others. You can do this through your communication, as well. How? Be genuine about connecting. Lead with empathy and concern, if required in a situation. Be as warm, open, and likeable as you can (without forcing yourself to be someone "different!").

Be a collaborative leader

Women are also known for being more collaborative than men. Where possible, include as many different viewpoints as possible, and encourage those who wouldn't normally speak up to contribute. You may also want to consider who the silent stakeholders are in the room: Who would want to know what's being discussed, or have a different viewpoint that needs to be included? Make sure to listen as much as possible while gathering feedback. Your teams will appreciate this!

Stand firm in conflict and only apologize when needed

Because women are generally seen as collaborators and peacemakers, we are often the first ones to compromise in a conflict. Don't be afraid to stand firm in conflict, especially if you feel strongly about your point of view. You may also try speaking in a firmer tone or louder than you are comfortable with to get your point across.

As women, we tend to over apologize. We apologize for everything and sometimes, we even apologize for things we have no control over! If you've hurt someone, do apologize. But don't apologize often just because. In addition, try not to apologize for everything. This weakens your apologies when they are warranted. Most things in business do not require an apology so when you notice yourself about to apologize ask yourself: Is this required or necessary to repair a relationship because of something I've done? If not, consider not apologizing and simply moving on.

Convey confidence with your body language

Part of strong communication is not only what you say but how you carry yourself. There are many ways that you can communicate authority and influence through your body language. For example, if you are shaking someone's hand make sure to have a firm handshake and look them directly in the eye.

You can also use body language to connect with another person. If the other person you are speaking with starts frowning, it may be a clue that they are not resonating with what you are saying. In addition, if they have their arms crossed, this could mean that they are feeling defensive and have put themselves in a protective stance. It could also mean that they simply are cold! It depends—but start by becoming aware of what the other person is doing while you are speaking and make sure to acknowledge anything that may add to your conversation.

Remain objective

Another stereotype is that women are overly emotional. This is often because we care. A lot! But, it's much better to remain objective in your communications. How do you do this? You separate your reactions from the communications, whenever possible. For example, perhaps something shocking just happened at work and your boss asks you how you're feeling. If you are close with your boss, you may feel comfortable sharing. However, it is absolutely ok to say you need some time to think about it and that you would like to discuss it soon. This allows you to gather your thoughts, feelings, and emotions, and to come back ready to have a meaningful discussion.

Don't stay on the sidelines

We've discussed before how important it is for you to raise your hand for new opportunities. This is especially important related to communications, too. Someone needs help following up? Raise your hand. A team needs one more person to present? Raise your hand. These small opportunities to work on communication skills *will* help you gain confidence over time. They will also be good opportunities to practise and potentially build new relationships across your organization or deepen relationships with those you already know well.

In Summary

There are many communications tips to consider if you are working on building your communications skills. The important thing is to understand the major differences in how men and women communicate with one another and to avoid communications pitfalls that may confuse or devalue what you have to say.

A successful female executive knows how to communicate directly to those who she works with—whether that is men, other women, clients, upper management, or otherwise. The background in this chapter has given you an overview of how men and women communicate differently and shows you what areas to focus on to increase your authority and display your confidence so that you can increase your influence with those you work with every day.

THE ART OF NEGOTIATION

Like strong communication, negotiation skills are not limited to the corporate world. You may not realize it, but each and every day you are already negotiating! You negotiate with others as you're passing them on the street, when scheduling things in a joint calendar with your partner, and sometimes, yes, even with your children.

Unfortunately, while you can take a class on negotiations and even specialize in it, there is no set path to becoming an expert negotiator. You'll also find that there are many books and opinions on how to negotiate. Some of this advice is helpful and others not as much. Also, some people love negotiating. It comes naturally for them. While others will have to work harder at refining those skills.

Regardless of where you fall on the scale of comfort levels with negotiation, if you want to advance in your career, you'll likely need to hone your negotiation skills at some point. Whether it's required in your job, negotiating on behalf of yourself (for example, when you get a new job), or negotiating on behalf of another (a direct report), these skills will help you navigate difficult situations that will arise throughout your career. Effective negotiation allows you to get what you want, which can help you reach your career goals even faster.

Negotiation Tactics

Gather as much information as possible

Before entering a negotiation, you'll want to prepare yourself for the discussion. Gather as much information as you can on the priorities of the other party. What are their goals? What does "winning" look like to them? You'll want to get an understanding of how they may respond to any of your requests. Knowing what their interests and motives are will help you understand what room exists for negotiation and how they communicate.

In addition, you'll want to do some simple research on the situation of the other party. Imagine yourself in their shoes, negotiating against you. Adam D. Galinsky, a professor at Northwestern's Kellogg School of Management wrote in the Harvard Business School's *Negotiation* newsletter: "The better able you are to get inside the head of your opponent, the better your negotiated outcomes are likely to be." For example, if you are in sales and are trying to sell a product to a company, you may want to ask questions like the following:

- Does this company currently use a product similar to ours?
- Why are they considering purchasing this product?
- How urgent is their need for the product?
- Is the person you're speaking with the decision-maker, or do other people need to sign off on it?
- What are the benefits for the other party?
- Do the benefits outweigh the costs for them? Do they feel like they are getting a good deal?
- What is their potential risk in the negotiation? What will they be looking out for?

It is also smart to research whether there is any history between the parties negotiating. If so, it may affect the thoughts and strategies of the other side as they enter into the negotiation. In addition, research your competitors so that you know what other products and services are available for purchase.

Other questions you may want to consider as you prepare for negotiation are questions that you can ask the other party before negotiating. You may want to consider asking questions like:

- Why are you interested in this purchase?
- What is your timeline for the purchase?
- What was your prior experience with [this product, service etc.]?
- What is most important about this for you today?

The questions you'll need to ask and the information you'll want to gather will vary depending on your unique situation. These questions should be a good starting point as you begin to prepare for a negotiation.

Know your alternatives

In addition to gathering as much information as possible, you'll want to know what your alternatives are before going into the negotiation. What is the best possible scenario if you do not do this deal? What alternatives do you have? This is called your best alternative to a negotiated agreement (or, BATNA for short). The term was coined by authors Roger Fisher and William Ury in their 1991 book *Getting to Yes*.

By determining what your alternatives are and what other options exist you strengthen your resolve to walk away if the deal goes in another direction. We'll talk more about walking away from the deal as another negotiation tactic later in this chapter.

Always ask for more than you want

Negotiations are like a dance; there is give and take. Knowing this, you should always ask for more than you want and more than what you would expect the other party to give. This way, when the other party comes back with a counteroffer it will be between where you started and what you've asked for. Normally, it is right around the number that you wanted in the first place.

If you do not ask for more than what you want, you run the risk of getting even less than what you may need or want. Even if you are a negotiator that likes to play fair and be honest and transparent, ask for slightly more than what your desired amount is so that there is wiggle room for negotiation.

Make your first offer real and enticing

Historically it was thought that it was best to let the other side take the lead in determining a starting offer point. However, if you are in a position where you can be the first mover you can use this position to your advantage by making the first offer.

If you know what price the other side has in mind, whether it is a range or a specific number, then you can make your offer slightly more than that. This will grab their attention. Why? Because it is close to what they were already expecting. It's also close to where they potentially thought you would mutually end up, which could speed up the process of the negotiation.

If you take this tactic, make your offer a real one. This means to not be outrageous in your request. Don't throw out such a huge number that it offends the other side.

Consider presenting multiple options and offers

One easy way to get feedback quickly is to offer multiple proposals or offers at once. This will allow you to gauge what's important to the other side. What do they like among the various offers? By gathering this information, you may be able to create an even more enticing offer that didn't exist before.

In addition, through offering multiple offers you'll get a better sense of their taste for the dollar amount proposed. Whether they baulked at a higher or lower offer is important. Dig into *why*. Now you'll have a more realistic understanding of what their budget might be or what they may be willing to accept.

If you decide to go this route you might also consider making the offers more or less the same value and differentiating the benefits within each offer. This will help you determine what is most important to the other side and what may be driving their negotiation.

Know the standards

In every negotiation, there are standards or values of the other party which may play a direct or unspoken role in the process. For example, if you are negotiating with an environmental company but your product is not environmentally friendly, they may not be as interested in pursuing your product, or may not see the benefits related to the cost you are proposing as they are used to paying more for vendors that are better for the environment.

You can be prepared for these situations by researching the other party in advance. Knowing what issues or causes are important to them or which might come up throughout the negotiation will help you prepare for any objections in advance. Find ways to not only address the potential concerns of the other party but that also help advance your goals. If you can also find quotes or reasoning that the other party has publicly shared (for example, the reasons they use a certain product or service) then you may even want to frame the benefits for them in your negotiation through this lens. For instance, if a CEO goes on record to say that they use a certain product for its efficiency then you may want to address that you understand efficiency is important to them and show how your product or service will make them even more efficient.

If, however, your product or service does not fall into the reasonings or rationales that the other party has deemed important, you'll want to explain clearly why an exception should be made in this particular instance.

Use body language to convey an emotion

Often, during a negotiation, an offer will be placed on the table (literally or figuratively). If you are unhappy with the offer, you can use your body language to say so. In this case, you may lean back and cross your arms or visibly flinch to show shock. You want to make sure that any body language you use is authentic to you. You don't want to appear as though you are acting. Nobody likes to negotiate unfairly. However, body language can help you in negotiation and convey your emotions and thoughts if used strategically.

Negotiation Tactics

Gather as much information as possible

Before entering a negotiation, you'll want to prepare yourself for the discussion. Gather as much information as you can on the priorities of the other party. What are their goals? What does "winning" look like to them? You'll want to get an understanding of how they may respond to any of your requests. Knowing what their interests and motives are will help you understand what room exists for negotiation and how they communicate.

In addition, you'll want to do some simple research on the situation of the other party. Imagine yourself in their shoes, negotiating against you. Adam D. Galinsky, a professor at Northwestern's Kellogg School of Management wrote in the Harvard Business School's *Negotiation* newsletter: "The better able you are to get inside the head of your opponent, the better your negotiated outcomes are likely to be." For example, if you are in sales and are trying to sell a product to a company, you may want to ask questions like the following:

- Does this company currently use a product similar to ours?
- Why are they considering purchasing this product?
- How urgent is their need for the product?
- Is the person you're speaking with the decision-maker, or do other people need to sign off on it?
- What are the benefits for the other party?
- Do the benefits outweigh the costs for them? Do they feel like they are getting a good deal?
- What is their potential risk in the negotiation? What will they be looking out for?

It is also smart to research whether there is any history between the parties negotiating. If so, it may affect the thoughts and strategies of the other side as they enter into the negotiation. In addition, you'll want to do research on your competitors so that you know what other products and services are available for purchase.

Other questions you may want to consider as you prepare for negotiation are questions that you can ask the other party before negotiating. You may want to consider asking questions like:

- Why are you interested in this purchase?
- What is your timeline for the purchase?
- What was your prior experience with [this product, service etc.]?
- What is most important about this for you today?

The questions you'll need to ask and the information you'll want to gather will vary depending on your unique situation. These questions should be a good starting point as you begin to prepare for a negotiation.

Know your alternatives

In addition to gathering as much information as possible, you'll want to know what your alternatives are before going into the negotiation. What is the best possible scenario if you do not do this deal? What alternatives do you have? This is called your best alternative to negotiated agreement (or, BATNA for short). The term was coined by authors Roger Fisher and William Ury in their 1991 book *Getting to Yes*.

By determining what your alternatives are and what other options exist you strengthen your resolve to walk away if the deal goes in another direction. We'll talk more about walking away from the deal as another negotiation tactic later in this chapter.

Always ask for more than you want

Negotiations are like a dance; there is give and take. Knowing this, you should always ask for more than you want and more than what you would expect the other party to give. This way, when the other party comes back with a counteroffer it will be between where you started and what you've asked for. Normally, it is right around the number that you wanted in the first place.

If you do not ask for more than what you want, you run the risk of getting even less than what you may need or want. Even if you are a negotiator that likes to play fair and be honest and transparent, ask for slightly more than what your desired amount is so that there is wiggle room for negotiation.

Make your first offer real and enticing

Historically it was thought that it was best to let the other side take the lead in determining a starting offer point. However, if you are in a position where you can be the first mover you can use this position to your advantage by making the first offer.

If you know what price the other side has in mind, whether it is a range or a specific number, then you can make your offer slightly more than that. This will grab their attention. Why? Because it is close to what they were already expecting. It's also close to where they potentially thought you would mutually end up, which could speed up the process of the negotiation.

If you take this tactic, make your offer a real one. This means to not be outrageous in your request. Don't throw out such a huge number that it offends the other side.

Consider presenting multiple options and offers

One easy way to get feedback quickly is to offer multiple proposals or offers at once. This will allow you to gauge what's important to the other side. What do they like among the various offers? By gathering this information, you may be able to create an even more enticing offer that didn't exist before.

In addition, through offering multiple offers you'll get a better sense of their taste for the dollar amount proposed. Whether they baulked at a higher or lower offer is important. Dig into *why*. Now you'll have a more realistic understanding of what their budget might be or what they may be willing to accept.

If you decide to go this route you might also consider making the offers more or less the same value and differentiating the benefits within each offer. This will help you determine what is most important to the other side and what may be driving their negotiation.

Know the standards

In every negotiation, there are standards or values of the other party which may play a direct or unspoken role in the process. For example, if you are negotiating with an environmental company but your product is not environmentally friendly, they may not be as interested in pursuing your product, or may not see the benefits related to the cost you are proposing as they are used to paying more for vendors that are better for the environment.

You can be prepared for these situations by researching the other party in advance. Knowing what issues or causes are important to them or which might come up throughout the negotiation will help you prepare for any objections in advance. Find ways to not only address the potential concerns of the other party but that also help advance your goals. If you can also find quotes or reasoning that the other party has publicly shared (for example, the reasons they use a certain product or service) then you may even want to frame the benefits for them in your negotiation through this lens. For instance, if a CEO goes on record to say that they use a certain product for its efficiency then you may want to address that you understand efficiency is important to them and show how your product or service will make them even more efficient.

If, however, your product or service does not fall into the reasonings or rationales that the other party has deemed important, you'll want to explain clearly why an exception should be made in this particular instance.

Use body language to convey an emotion

Often, during a negotiation, an offer will be placed on the table (literally or figuratively). If you are unhappy with the offer, you can use your body language to say so. In this case, you may lean back and cross your arms or visibly flinch to show shock. You want to make sure that any body language you use is authentic to you. You don't want to appear as though you are acting. Nobody likes to negotiate unfairly. However, body language can help you in negotiation and convey your emotions and thoughts if used strategically.

You'll know if this tactic worked in how the other party responds to it. If they see your flinch or crossing of your arms and they don't immediately offer a concession or change the offer, it may be the best they can do. However, most people will want to address your reactions and may adjust accordingly (for example, by changing an offer or asking what your objections are to it).

Practice

For many people, negotiations can be stressful and anxiety-inducing. You can develop confidence in your negotiation skills by practising as much as possible. Practice makes perfect. When you're ready, start practising your negotiations over and over. You can do this while looking at yourself in the mirror, or recording yourself on your phone or computer and playing it back. You can also practise with a friend who is willing to provide feedback.

Look for ways that you can practise throughout your day as well. For example, you could negotiate at the grocery store if a piece of produce is damaged by asking for a discount. If you need a flexible schedule due to a personal matter you can consider asking your boss as a negotiation rather than simply a question. If you're in a buying capacity at work, you can ask your vendors for discounts.

When counter-offering, present a strong offer

If you are unable to present the first offer and "anchor" the negotiation, then make sure to present a strong counteroffer when you do so. If you are not sure where to start you can consider counter-offering with what would have been your first offer.

If your original offer is wildly different than what the other party first proposed, consider revising but remember to check in with the information you've gathered previously and check against your BATNA. Then, with confidence, present an offer that you believe is fair to both parties.

If you feel that the other side is not taking you as seriously, you may want to strategically disclose what your BATNA is. They may then understand that your offer is strong and real and be more inclined to take it. If you decide to do this, make sure to use this tactic strategically and not to disclose too early.

Always be prepared to walk away

The real power in a negotiation is in knowing what you will *not* accept. It's called "walking away." Let's say that a negotiation is going south, and the other party is not being receptive to anything you are suggesting. Rather than get frustrated or flustered, simply walk away. Be professional and grateful for the time they took to vet out this opportunity with you but be confident that this is not the right situation for you. It also allows you to protect the value of your product or service by preventing you from discounting too greatly.

When you know that, worst-case scenario, you can walk away and start again with someone else at a later point in time, you'll gain the confidence to negotiate confidently. Nobody wins in every negotiation throughout their entire life. In those situations that simply cannot meet your standards, you can confidently walk away knowing another opportunity that more closely aligns with what you need and want will come along.

Spoken and unspoken rules of negotiation

Now that we know the tactics to use while negotiating, we can focus on rules of negotiation that can be used to our advantage. It's also helpful to know what the unspoken rules are if you are newer to negotiating. These are things that experienced negotiators may well understand but unless someone points them out to you, you may not be aware of them.

Rule #1: Everything is negotiable

Let's say for instance that you are buying a car. You may think that the price is the piece that you'd negotiate. But did you also know that *everything* is negotiable? You can negotiate not only a price reduction, but perhaps you'd like an oil change, a new air filter, new windshield wipers put on, and a car wash before taking that car home.

In life, everything is negotiable. In our day and age, more and more people are working from home. But it wasn't always like that. If something is bothering you, like an imbalance in your work schedule, or if you'd like some more breathing room on the weekends, think of it as a negotiation. How can you bring it up in a way that you make it a win-win? Perhaps you take fewer shifts this week and a colleague who has been asking for more work fills in. Or, you take on more work throughout the week so that you can have more hours back to yourself on the weekends. Don't be afraid to get creative with potential solutions! You may not always get what you want but it will not be due to a lack of effort.

MAKING FEAR WORK FOR YOU

If you think that successful people never feel fear, then you are mistaken. Take a look at the quotes below from extremely successful women and their thoughts on fear:

"I put one of my biggest worries into When Harry Met Sally, which was that I would move to New York and nothing would become of me, and I would die in my apartment and no one would notice until the smell drifted out into the hallway. I have a very clear memory of standing in Central Park when I was in college and looking at all those buildings that surrounded the park and just thinking, 'Am I ever going to know anyone here?' I mean, that moment when you first come to New York and you don't know

anyone. ... But as a kid, you're just overwhelmed by just how badly you want to come here and how frightening it is that nothing will happen to you. You know, that all this ambition would be for nothing."

— NORA EPHRON, AUTHOR

"Fearlessness is like a muscle. I know from my own life that the more I exercise it the more natural it becomes to not let my fears run me."

— ARIANNA HUFFINGTON

"When you're a CEO, you can't break too many stereotypical expectations. I wish you could, but you can't ... every morning you've got to wake up with a healthy fear that the world is changing, and a conviction that, to win, you have to change faster and be more agile than anyone else."

— INDRA NOOYI, FORMER
CHAIRPERSON AND CEO OF PEPSICO

"College was probably the most impactful thing that I have done in my life other than being the First Lady and having kids and marrying Barack Obama. ... It taught me that I could leave home and be successful away from home. It taught me how to open up, how to try new things that are scary, how to buck expectations and beat the odds, and all that good stuff. ... Just try new things. Don't be afraid. Step out of your comfort zones and soar, all right?"

— MICHELLE OBAMA

Every person, and yes, even extremely successful women feel fear. However, they can harness this fear and use courage to push through the barriers and walls that make us comfortable and keeps us fearful. Let's take a look at how other successful women have overcome fear generally and then we'll address overcoming specific fears you may find in the workplace.

Overcoming fear generally

Often, we feel fear related to a situation because there is some level of uncertainty. We are unsure of how things will play out and scared of what we do not know. Here are tips to help you break through and overcome fear when you're not sure how to move forward.

Be true and honest with yourself

Remember what makes you unique and what value you bring to the table. Margaret Mitchell, President, and CEO of YWCA in Greater Cleveland in a blog[1] suggests knowing your strengths, weaknesses, and professional desire at all times. This will help guide your decisions as you move throughout your career. This also helps you thrive in areas where you are strong and allows you to empower others whose strengths may complement your weaknesses.

Focus on the end goal

What is your "why" for coming to work every day? How is this fear either a progression and sign of growth of your reasons for coming into the office or a detractor from it? If you work for a company with a mission statement, think about the impact you are generating each day. Is this fear greater than those customers or people that would be helped by you pushing through it? Sometimes when we look at things through this lens, we can overcome our fear and turn it into courage.

Accept being uncomfortable

If you are growing and pushing yourself outside of your comfort zone you will naturally experience fear. Why? Because the situation is new! Your brain has not had time to reconcile how it will process this new experience and fear shows up because we don't know how the situation will turn out.

If you can get comfortable with being uncomfortable. Acknowledging that most people feel fear and take action anyway can be extremely powerful. Knowing that you are not alone and that these feelings are normal can often be just what someone needs to push through.

Overcoming the fear of becoming an entrepreneur

If you have ever had a full-time job and wondered whether you're ready to make the leap to entrepreneur full-time, I would imagine that you felt some level of fear with the decision. This is normal. Our jobs are supposed to provide stability. Being an entrepreneur is extremely rewarding and yet, the thought of it can produce anxiety and fear in even the strongest person.

Tracy Nour, Founder of SheJustKnows, says the following about this leap: "Leaving a reliable, senior position at a multi-billion dollar company to start something on my own with no real concrete plan was terrifying. I knew I could really set myself back in my career while disappointing myself and those I love. Even though I was afraid, I did everything I possibly could to make sure it would work out. I listened to what people needed from me, I hustled daily, I treated people well and I delivered great work. It was the hardest thing I ever did, but I am a better person because of it."

If you're working on overcoming this fear, consider the following:

- Prepare for everything! Plan as much as you can.
- Have a backup in case things do not work out.
- Ask questions to those who have been in your shoes before.
- Work hard. Focus entirely on your goal and do not stop until you see progress!
- Ensure your product or service is top-notch.

You can also list out your fears and write affirmations or responses addressing them to alleviate fears.

Overcoming the fear of saying 'No'

Nobody likes disappointing others, and for most women generally, relationships are important. However, some people struggle with a very real fear around saying 'No.' Danielle Gano, Founder/CEO of Elle.com, says: "Learning to say no is a process I'm still working through, but it's started to become easier as a result of better considering my motivations for agreeing to things. Thinking carefully about my intentions for why I would say yes or no to a request has given me a better model for evaluating when I should learn to say no, and also reduced my fears about disappointing others or missing out on opportunities."

If saying 'No' to someone is fearful you may want to ask yourself why that is so. Are you afraid that you're not working hard enough for this individual? Perhaps you are afraid of the perception that it may give? Here are additional tips to work through this fear:

- Instead of thinking of it as saying 'No' to someone, think of it as saying 'Yes' to your priorities.
- If you don't know what your priorities are, make a list, and stick to them. Once you've defined them you may feel more comfortable declining items that are not on the list.
- Vet out your motivations, as Danielle suggests. Sometimes there is an opportunity that you simply feel strongly about which you may want to say 'Yes' to. In that case, you may need to remove something else from your plate. Give yourself the flexibility and permission to do so.

Overcoming the fear of asking for help

As women in business, we often feel that we need to do it all, and be everything to everyone. It's a well-known fact that women have had to work harder than men over time to get a seat at the table. Charlotte Winton, the former mayor of Ottawa and first woman mayor of a Canadian city was quoted as saying: "Whatever women do, they must do twice as well as men to be thought half as good. Luckily, this is not difficult." Because women often feel the need to prove themselves, it can be extremely hard to admit when we need help. Cait Fraser, Co-Founder of Wanderwell, says: "I wanted to be able to 'Do it all,' but this just led to more anxiety, burnout and loss of self-esteem. I overcame this fear when I was on a retreat and each person had to ask for something that they need help with. This was an incredible 'aha' moment. I saw that I was not alone and that every successful entrepreneur gets to where they are because they ask for help."

People at the top of the business organization did not get there alone. Often, they got there because others helped them along the way. Remember that you were hired into your role because you have expertise in one or more areas. If you find yourself focused on things outside of these priorities, you may consider asking for help in those areas where others can easily step in and the end result would be the same. This allows you to focus on where you can make your largest impact on an organization.

Overcoming the fear of being in the spotlight

If you are successful enough, eventually your "brand" will be public. This means people in and outside of your industry might become aware of you. For some people, there is a very real fear around this. Especially if you are a private person. The internet can emphasize these fears. You potentially open yourself up to criticism and become vulnerable to judgment in a much different way online than in real life.

Shira Lenchewski, MS, RD, author, and Founder of ShiraRD had a fear related to this: "At my core I'm exceptionally private, so putting myself out there on social media for my career was a major fear of mine. I overcame it by figuring out what I was actually afraid of: misrepresenting myself. The truth is as long as we show up as ourselves the world will generally respond positively, and we can achieve even more than we thought possible. The more authentic we can be, the better. I have to remind myself that I worked long and hard to get where I am today, and I shouldn't be afraid to share my knowledge and skills with others!"

When you take the focus off of yourself and put it in light of helping others with knowledge and skills that they might not otherwise have, then you allow yourself an opportunity to overcome this fear. Lenchewski's advice to stay true to who you are and to be authentic will allow you to resonate deeply with those who appreciate these traits. This will allow you to be even more impactful as you connect with others in the public sphere.

Overcoming the fear of not being liked

We've mentioned again and again throughout this book how important relationships are to women. Along with that comes the desire to be liked. It's only natural to want to have strong relationships with no conflict. However, a fear of not being liked can prevent women from saying what needs to be said or from setting boundaries for their own wellbeing simply because they feel like they will be shunned. To advance in your career you must stay true to yourself and become comfortable with not being liked.

Maggie Neilson, CEO of the Global Group used to have a fear about not being liked: "Especially early on in my career, I wanted to be liked by everyone. Now I've realized that there has to be a hard line between the personal and the professional. It is my job – and in everyone's best interests – for me to deliver hard news at times ranging from performance feedback to even employment termination. I see now that reasonable minds can disagree, and I'm never going to be able to convince everyone of my perspective, nor are they going to have access to all of the factors at play and that is ok."

In your job, you want to make sure that you are being respectful of others but as Neilson alludes to, do not confuse the need to be liked by allowing yourself to make poor business decisions or letting an unsatisfactory work product slide. What matters most is that people respect you, not that they like you. Remember that we are all human so there is no reason to be unnecessarily harsh. Treat everyone the way you would want to be treated, especially in difficult conversations or situations.

Overcoming a fear of failure

Failure. The big "F." Nobody likes to fail. Vitina Blumenthal, founder of WonderfulSoul says about failure: "Failing does not have to be something we are terrified of, but for years I have let negative thoughts eat away at me. For me, learning to catch my mind when self-sabotaging thoughts come up has been the best skill I've learned to date. It doesn't necessarily mean that 'negative' thoughts don't come up. It just makes it easier to get through low periods quicker, while still staying productive and moving forward." Often, our fear of failure can be traced back to how we as children were raised.

In an article[2] written by Felena Hanson for Ellevate Network titled *Three Ways Women Can Turn Fear of Failure into Fearless Action*, Hanson says that much of how women view perfectionism and success (and, by extension, also a fear of failure) stems from our childhood. Hanson states that as young girls we are encouraged to be nice and to get along with everyone. That, combined with the idea that success comes from external factors outside of ourselves (which she labels as an "external locus of control"), means that women strive for perfection. We don't want to fail for fear of what it could mean about *us*, whereas as young boys, men learn through failure.

Hanson mentions that to step outside of this need for perfection and external validation we need to embrace fearlessness, which we build by making "decisions outside of our comfort zone." She says there are three ways to do this: 1) Finding examples to emulate, 2) Owning our achievements and resilience, and 3) Confidently pushing ourselves.

Finding examples to emulate

Think of successful women who you admire and ask yourself: what qualities do this person have that I'd like to emulate? You can make a list of qualities that you would like to work towards if you do not already have them.

It is important to recognize that the people that you admire also felt fear and still became successful! If it helps, read more about how they got to where they are and the obstacles and adversity that they each overcame. This may give you the courage to continue to step outside of your comfort zone and take action even if you feel fear in your day-to-day.

Recognize your achievements and resilience

Sometimes as women we can simply be too hard on ourselves. Especially people who are achiever-types or who always have another goal that they would like to hit. If this sounds like you, make sure you take time regularly to acknowledge your achievements. You'll also want to acknowledge the adversity that you've overcome. We referenced keeping a happy folder or brag book earlier in this book and these can be places of respite for when you need a reminder of the wonderful things that you've accomplished over time. Remember the times when you felt fear, moved forward, and came out stronger on the other side.

Brené Brown acknowledges that sometimes we don't want to acknowledge our fear because it's uncomfortable: "We're so self critical, and….there is an ideal of what you're supposed to be. And what a lot of us end up doing is we orphan the parts of ourselves that don't fit with that ideal of who we're supposed to be." However, banishing fear from your life is not possible. We've already mentioned that you are not alone in this feeling; everyone feels fear.

When you're feeling fear one tactic could be to acknowledge it, feel it, and then remember how you've pushed past it before. Remember that you've been successful before, and you can do it again. You can feel the fear and do it anyway.

Trust your talents enough to push you

In her article for Ellevate Network, Hanson mentions that according to a 2017 American Express Open Report,[3] only 3% of female founders ever break the million-dollar mark in annual sales. Hanson argues that this is due to women being less likely to take a calculated risk, despite women's businesses growing rapidly over time as a whole.

Hanson says that we need to surround ourselves with people who will encourage us to grow. This could apply to your business and also to you. Do you have people in your life who are encouraging you to move forward, push past limiting beliefs, and grow? Hanson writes: "There are significant resources and infinite possibilities in the world; we have to believe we are good enough to not only claim them but also to run after them."

Hanson states that we as women should listen to our intuition, which often knows what the best next move is for each of us individually. Trust in yourself and your talents, and when you start to doubt, lean on those in your life who can lovingly encourage you to move beyond your comfort zone.

In Summary

The fear of failure will often stop someone from succeeding before they even start. It is not that the most successful women in business do not feel fear. It is just that they have learned to be uncomfortable and to move forward *anyway*. Hopefully, you took away tips in this chapter that will help you turn fear into courage and move forward, especially if you have been stuck. Strengthen your "fearlessness" muscle by regularly doing things outside of your comfort zone. If you are struggling and in need of encouragement, look back to past accomplishments and how you managed to harness your prior fear and succeed anyway. Your life experience is your own best case study and proof that you can succeed and you will succeed—even despite any fear you may feel in the moment.

CONCLUSION

If you've made it this far you are well on your way to understanding what it takes to be a successful female leader. Hopefully, some themes and topics resonated with you no matter where you are in your career trajectory. I hope you've learned by now that success is not a blueprint that you can simply follow and arrive at the desired destination (the top). If only it were that simple! Your career will require you to gain new skills each and every day, but this book has addressed many that are necessary to become successful in business.

As a quick recap, you now know the following:

- Chapter 1: The personality traits of the most successful women
- Chapter 2: How to identify and hone your personal style of leadership

- Chapter 3: How to solve problems and challenges that may arise throughout your career
- Chapter 4: How to develop a high-performing team
- Chapter 5: How to overcome imposter syndrome and self-doubt
- Chapter 6: Building self-confidence in yourself and others
- Chapter 7: Tips for stronger communication skills
- Chapter 8: The art of negotiation
- Chapter 9: Making fear work for you

As a next step to reading this book, I would recommend that you listen to the nudges you received while reading. Are there areas that you feel you need to focus or work on? Anything that you think would help you get to the next step in your career? Once you've determined what those areas are, create an action plan to help you practise and implement new skills. Then, make sure to measure your progress over time and celebrate any wins. This will keep you motivated over time as the journey to climbing the corporate ladder can be a long and slow one.

Another important thing to remember is that we do not get to the top alone. Where possible, help others out along the way. Share the information that you've learned here and lead by example in the office. Younger women, especially those early on in their careers, will be watching and imitating you—whether or not you may be aware of it!

It is my dream to get this into the hands of as many women as possible. I sincerely hope that you have enjoyed reading this book and that it resonated with you. If it did, please feel free to share it with others and if you would consider leaving a review on Amazon, I would greatly appreciate it.

What kind of a leader are you?

Find out your leadership style in 2 minutes!

TAKE THE QUIZ

Visit

www.shethinkslikeaboss.com

to take our quiz, find out what type of leader you are today!

REFERENCES

Pew Research Center. (2018, September 20). *Views on leadership traits and competencies and how they intersect with gender.* https://www.pewresearch.org/social-trends/2018/09/20/2-views-on-leadership-traits-and-competencies-and-how-they-intersect-with-gender/.

Inc. (2018, February 2). *Tony Robbins on the psychology and skills of exceptional leaders* [Video]. YouTube https://www.youtube.com/watch?v=mBNoUhHtmVc.

Comparably. (2018, March 28). *Study: The worst traits in a boss.* https://www.comparably.com/blog/study-the-worst-traits-in-a-boss/.

Wilkins, M. M. (2014, November 11). *Signs that you're a micromanager.* Harvard Business Review. https://hbr.org/2014/11/signs-that-youre-a-micromanager.

Pew Research Center. (2015, January 14). *Chapter 1: Women in leadership.* https://www.pewresearch.org/social-trends/2015/01/14/chapter-1-women-in-leadership/.

KPMG. (2020, October). *Advancing the future of women in business.* https://womensleadership.kpmg.us/content/dam/womensleadership/pdf/2020/2020wlsstudy.pdf.

Keller, K. (n.d.). *Women influencing business: Using your problem solving skills.* Keller Institute. https://www.kellerinstitute.com/content/women-influencing-business-using-your-problem-solving-skills.

Simplilearn. (2020, June 1). *The secret recipe to building high performance teams.* https://www.simplilearn.com/building-high-performing-teams-article.

Torppa, C. B. (2010, February 25). *Gender issues: Communication differences in interpersonal relationships.* Ohioline Ohio University Extension. https://ohioline.osu.edu/factsheet/FLM-FS-4-02-R10.

Keller, S., Meaney, M. (2017, June 28). *High performing teams: A timeless leadership topic.* McKinsey & Company. https://www.mckinsey.com/business-functions/organization/our-insights/high-performing-teams-a-timeless-leadership-topic.

Folkman, J. (2016, April 13). *5 ways to build a high performance team.* Forbes. https://www.forbes.com/sites/

joefolkman/2016/04/13/are-you-on-the-team-from-hell-5-ways-to-create-a-high-performance-team/?sh=5938296d7ee2.

Corporate Finance Institute. (n.d.). *SMART goal.* https://corporatefinanceinstitute.com/resources/knowledge/other/smart-goal/.

Baldoni, J. (2008, June 23). *Motivation disconnect: How organizations fail to motivate managers.* Harvard Business Review. https://hbr.org/2008/06/motivation-disconnect-how-orga.

IDG Research Services. (2012). *The gender divide: What motivates employees.* [Infographic]. https://cpb-us-w2.wpmucdn.com/blog.nus.edu.sg/dist/a/3546/files/2014/02/IDG-Research-Gender-Infographic-19o9omd.jpg.

Clance, P.R., Imes, S. (n.d.). The imposter phenomenon in high achieving women: Dynamics and therapeutic intervention. *UpToDate.* Retrieved April 16, 2021, from https://www.paulineroseclance.com/pdf/ip_high_achieving_women.pdf.

Columbia Business School. (2011, November 28). *Men's honest overconfidence may lead to male domination in the c-suite.* https://www8.gsb.columbia.edu/newsroom/newsn/1879/mens-honest-overconfidence-may-lead-to-male-domination-in-the-csuite.

Burey, J., Tulshyan, R. (2021, February 11). *Stop telling women they have imposter syndrome.* Harvard Business Review.

https://hbr.org/2021/02/stop-telling-women-they-have-imposter-syndrome.

Kay, K., Shipman, C. (2014 May). *The confidence gap*. The Atlantic. https://www.theatlantic.com/magazine/archive/2014/05/the-confidence-gap/359815/.

Ayduk, O., & Bremner, R., & Bruehlman-Senecal, E., & Burson, A., & Dougherty, A., & Kross, E., & Moser, J., & Park, J., & Shablack, H. (2012). Self-talk as a regulatory mechanism: How you do it matters. *American Psychological Association Journal of Personality and Social Psychology, 106*(2), 304-324. http://dx.doi.org/10.1037/a0035173.

Artabane, M., Coffman, J., Darnell, D. (2017, January 31). *Charting the course: Getting women to the top*. Bain & Company. https://www.bain.com/insights/charting-the-course-women-on-the-top.

Bennett, J. (2014, April 22). *It's not you, it's science: How perfectionism holds women back*. Time. https://time.com/70558/its-not-you-its-science-how-perfectionism-holds-women-back/.

Babcock, L., Laschever, S. (n.d.). *Women don't ask: Negotiation and the gender divide*. Princeton University Press. https://press.princeton.edu/books/hardcover/9780691089409/women-dont-ask.

Robbins, M. (2018, February 20). *7 ways women can display more confidence at work.* https://melrobbins.com/7-ways-women-can-display-confidence-work/.

Catalyst. (2004). *Women and men in u.s. corporate leadership.* https://www.catalyst.org/wp-content/uploads/2019/02/Women-and_Men_in_U.S._Corporate_Leadership_Same_Workplace_Different_Realities.pdf.

Brescoll, V. (2012). Who takes the floor and why: Gender, power, and volubility in organizations. [Abstract]. *Administrative Science Quarterly, 56*(4), 622-641. https://doi.org/10.1177/0001839212439994.

Decker, K. (n.d.). *Pause. Just pause.* Decker Communications. https://decker.com/blog/pause-just-pause/.

Shonk, K. (2021, March 18). *What is a win-win negotiation?.* Harvard Business Review. https://www.pon.harvard.edu/daily/win-win-daily/what-is-a-win-win-negotiation/.

Mitchell, M. (2017, December 28). *Overcoming fear is essential to effective leadership.* Smart Business. https://www.sbnonline.com/article/overcoming-fear-is-essential-to-effective-leadership/.

Hanson, F. (n.d.). *Three ways women can turn fear of failure into fearless action.* Ellevate. https://www.ellevatenetwork.

com/articles/9457-three-ways-women-can-turn-fear-of-failure-into-fearless-action.

American Express. (n.d.). *State of women-owned businesses report.* https://www.americanexpress.com/en-us/business/trends-and-insights/keywords/state-of-women-owned-businesses-report/.

CPSIA information can be obtained
at www.ICGtesting.com
Printed in the USA
LVHW082211071022
730130LV00003B/407